Bill Beshear

PERSIAN CATS
and other LONGHAIRS

by JEANNE A. RAMSDALE

Assisted by

PHILIP N. RAMSDALE, D.V.M.

Distributed in the U.S.A. by T.F.H. Publications, Inc., 211 West Sylvania Avenue, P.O. Box 27, Neptune City, N.J. 07753; in England by I.F.H. (Gt. Britain) Ltd., 13 Nutley Lane, Reigate, Surrey; in Canada to the book store and library trade by Clarke, Irwin & Company, Clarwin House, 791 St. Clair Avenue West, Toronto 10, Ontario; in Canada to the pet trade by Rolf C. Hagen Ltd., 3225 Sartelon Street, Montreal 382, Quebec; in Southeast Asia by Y.W. Ong, 9 Lorong 36 Geylang, Singapore 14; in Australia and the south Pacific by Pet Imports Pty. Ltd., P.O. Box 149, Brookvale 2100, N.S.W., Australia. Published by T.F.H. Publications, Inc. Ltd., The British Crown-Crown Colony of Hong Kong.

ACKNOWLEDGEMENTS

I am deeply indebted to those who generously shared the knowledge gained from their experiences, and contributed their valuable photographs.

The benefit from the assistance given by my husband, Philip N. Ramsdale, Doctor of Veterinary Medicine, cannot be measured, but is gratefully acknowledged.

ISBN 0-87666-179-7

CONTENTS

mites, Ticks, Maggots, Insect Bites . . . Viral Diseases and Vaccinations: Rabies, Feline Enteritis, Pneumonitis and Other Respiratory Infections . . . How to Give a Pill or Capsule . . . How to Give Liquid Medication

PART TWO

Author and friends. Photo by Hans Bomskow.

*This book is dedicated to all
the cats who helped me write it.*

FOREWORD

In owning and caring for a fine Persian cat, you have the extra satisfaction of knowing that its beauty and charm will reflect *your* attention and love as well as its original background.

It is hoped that this book will serve as a general guide to a more complete knowledge and understanding of the requirements for raising a healthy, beautiful animal. Cats are individualistic, and there are many exceptions to any rules that have been formulated for them.

Further information on specific subjects may be obtained by consultation with the owner of your pet-supply store, cat breeder, and veterinarian, each of whom is expert in his field.

Beautiful longhairs give the appearance of being dressed in elegant fur clothing.

THE LUSCIOUS LONGHAIRS
An Introduction Is in Order

Persian cats give the impression they are dressed to attend an affair for the socially elite. Their fur coats, as lushly elegant as milady's mink, seem to connote a prestige rank in the world of cats, and their aristocratic mien lends elegance to whatever surroundings they grace.

The eyes of a Persian cat are the focal point of his beauty. They resemble brilliant jewels of a shade chosen to complement his costume. His large, round, wide-set eyes and short snub nose above a seemingly smiling mouth create a picture of appealing innocence.

Besides having an appearance of high quality, his manner, befitting his lineage, is dignified and gracious, with just a hint of restraint to discourage undue familiarity on the part of strangers.

Although a Persian may give the impression that he is slow-moving, he can surprise you with his speed when the occasion demands. If haste is not required, he does not go out of his way to exert himself.

To best enjoy the presence of a Persian in your home, it is necessary to know and understand his individual nature and the proper way to care for his physical needs. The Persian is not a fragile animal. Under his fancy dress is a sturdy, compact body. His muscular system is so well designed that he can keep in trim by little more exercise than a few daily stretches. This makes him an ideal house pet. However, a Persian does require extra attention to his coat, and the little care required to maintain it is a small price to pay for the reward in beauty.

Persians usually are gentle and quietly affectionate in temperament. Many of them are very dependent upon, and desirous of, human companionship. Of course, any affectionate demonstrations, such as head-butting, cuddling, and lap-sitting, occur only at their convenience, a characteristic common to all cats.

Whether you choose a male or a female will make no difference in your potential enjoyment of a Persian. Both sexes are equally lovable in their own special way. Males usually are larger, more impressive in appearance, and more boisterous. Females are more delicate in their beauty and have "girlish ways." However, some males are less aggressive than might be expected; likewise, some females are tomboys.

There is a wide variety of colors to choose from in the Persian cat family. Each color has been developed and perfected to striking beauty. In the United States today, on the basis of the number currently being registered with the Cat Fanciers Association, the most popular colors, in this order, are: Chinchilla and Shaded Silvers, Blue, White, and Black. However, each part of the country seems to have its own color preference. There have been 150,000 purebred cats of all breeds registered here since 1900. New registrations now average 15,000 per year.

Origins

No one has been able to determine how, where, or if the long-haired domestic cat emerged from the wild varieties of feline he resembles.

There is a wild Pallas cat that has long, soft fur. The coloring is yellowish-gray on top, with a lighter underside. There are some dark stripes on the very broad head and face and also on the hindquarters and tail. The present home of the Pallas cat is the high northern Asiatic desert area.

There are many varieties of lynxes and bobcats, all long-haired. Their fur is brown, marked with indistinct darker spots and lines, and, occasionally, white-speckled underneath. Lynxes have tufted ears, feet, and jowls, similar to today's Persians.

Now nearly extinct, with only a few still left in Scotland, is the European wildcat. Brownish, with stripes marking the long, bushy coat, this wildcat is approximately the size of the domestic cat.

A variety of long-haired domesticated cat much like our Persian has been found in Afghanistan for many years. It, too, is called Persian. Its origin is unknown.

The Angora is another variety of domesticated cat with a long coat, and its characteristics differ from the Persian's only slightly. Known in Turkey and Armenia, its name comes from the similarity of its fur to that of the Angora goat of the mountain province of Ankara, Turkey. Prior origins of the Angora cat also are unknown.

It is reasonable to suppose that Crusaders, seafarers, and other travelers to the East brought back some of these known long-haired domesticated cats when they returned to their native countries.

Latter-Day Persians

Over the years, long-haired cats have been admired by many notables for their beauty, grace, and charming companionship.

11

Attractive tributes to them have been made in well-known paintings, music, prose, and poetry in all parts of the world.

At the present time, long-haired cats, and particularly kittens, are used widely as photographic models. They well illustrate the intangibles of gentleness, softness, grace, elegance, charm, and goodness which may be associated with the products advertised. Beautiful actresses such as Jayne Mansfield and Joan Caulfield have found the Persian cat's beauty complementary to their own and have posed with them.

Some Persian cats have made a career out of being photographer's models, by themselves. Famous is Nicodemus, a Chinchilla Silver Persian, who supports his owner by posing with elegant furs, hats, and jewelry. He is in great demand and receives above-average modeling fees. Nicodemus, The Career Cat, is incorporated, and his name is copyrighted. Articles and stories about him have appeared in magazines all over the country.

At the turn of the century, those interested in the breeding and showing of cats began crossing the Angora and Persian varieties of longhairs. The Angora was characterized by a long, silky, fine-textured coat. The body and tail were long and slender; the head was small, with pointed, tufted ears, and a full mane, or ruff, extended down the chest to hang between the front legs. At that time, the most popular colors in Angoras were blue (maltese), white, and blue with white. Persians of that day had woolly, thick fur, but not as long and flowing as that of the Angora; however, their heads were broader and larger, ears smaller and more rounded, and body structure shorter and sturdier.

As time went on, the desired head and body type for a long-haired cat closely resembled that of the original Persian. The ideal coat was a blend of the Angora length and silkiness with the thickness of the Persian fur to give it more body and substance. The Angora has disappeared as a distinct breed, and the name has become obsolete. All the purebred longhairs now are properly called Persians and will be so called in this book.

The standard set forth for long-haired cats is a description of the mythical "perfect show cat," the ultimate that we strive for in breeding. No one cat has yet achieved perfection in every detail, but many very nearly do, and the general level continues to improve as more persons become interested in developing the fine points of each color variety. A scale of points is allotted to each of the individual features. Both the standard and the number of points vary slightly in some of the national organizations, but the requirements, basically, are the same in all.

The faults and objections that are mentioned seem to be tendencies to "throw back" to original ancestry in type and coloring, when nature, alone, had arranged an animal's coloring protectively, so that he would blend with his surroundings. If seen from above, his stripes or speckles would appear as the irregularities of the ground cover or leaf-dappled shade; if he were in a tree, and viewed from below, his lighter underside would blend better with the color of the sky. Likewise, his body and head were shaped so as to enable him to survive in the place in which he lived. As these challenges no longer are a factor, the emphasis is entirely on eye-appeal.

Through long years of selective breeding, certain standards for color patterns, or lack of them, in the recognized colors of longhairs have been set strictly on the basis of beauty. The desired eye color, as deep and intense a shade as possible, was evolved to assure the most effective contrast with coat color.

That the features of the Persian cat are thoroughly described and limits set forth, however, does not limit the variety of beauty possible within the standard. There is no way to standardize beauty; the many lovely pictures of show cats that illustrate this book are proof of this point.

I
PEDIGREE, NAMES, AND REGISTRATION

Pedigrees

There are two phases to the valid ownership of a purebred pedigreed cat. One, the pedigree itself; the other, the certificate of registration.

The pedigree is the record of your cat's parentage traced back for at least four generations to his sixteen great-great-grandparents. The certificate of registration is proof that his pedigree is correct, as well as the title of valid ownership. Each will be discussed separately, as they serve different purposes, although they are related.

A pedigree form starts with the full registered name of the sire (father), his championship status, registration number in one of the several cat-registering associations (referred to elsewhere), coat color, and eye color. The sire's ancestry is listed on the top half of the form. The same information for the dam (mother) is on the bottom half. In turn, the sire's sire and dam, and the dam's sire and dam, etc., are carried back as far as is necessary (usually four generations) to establish proof of continuous purebred ancestry. Each one's coat color, registration number, etc., is listed.

Should your cat, in turn, become the parent of a kitten, you could be called upon to write up this kitten's pedigree. To do so, insert your cat's name in the space provided for the sire or dam, as the case may be. Then copy the rest of your cat's pedigree into the sections following this. The other half of the kitten's pedigree is done in the same fashion, using the other parent's name and pedigree.

The foregoing is of great interest to anyone planning to breed to or from your cat. The cats in the pedigree usually are known to an experienced breeder, or their relatives are known, along

Holding a furry body close feels good to a child. Virginia Ramsdale and **BEVERLY-SERRANO ROGER.** Photo by Bomskow.

with the individual characteristics of each cat. A plan for strengthening (or attempting to eliminate) certain tendencies and improving future generations then can be projected, based on this information.

Included in the pedigree information is your own cat's breed, sex, coat color, eye color and date of birth. The name of the owner of the sire should be listed and her signature affixed if possible. The owner of the dam is the breeder of the kitten, and her name and signature must also appear for the pedigree to be authentic.

If any items of the record are lacking, there is a possibility that your cat or kitten will not be accepted for registration. It is important to check carefully the form you are given to make sure it is completely filled out.

Titles in the Pedigree

In the United States, there are six national organizations for the purpose of registering the names and pedigrees of purebred cats, both longhair and shorthair. These organizations also sanction shows and keep records of the wins made at the cat shows put on by their affiliated clubs. The rules and procedures of each national organization differ slightly, but are similar in all important respects. A cat may attain championship and grand championship status in any one association, or in all six associations. This accounts for the multiple championship title which often precedes the name of a cat that has been shown.

RM, standing for Royal Merit, preceding a cat's championship status in his title, is a special award given by the American Cat Fanciers' Association, and signifies that the cat's quality has been scored at their shows, above 95 (out of a possible 100) by at least seven of their judges. HM, or High Merit, is a comparable award of a slightly lower score. Since this association is relatively new, this type of rating does not appear for the older cats in the pedigree. Absence of such a rating for younger cats does not mean that they are poor quality, as not all cats are exhibited in all associations.

Names

Choosing a formal name for your kitten is the next step toward registration, after you have obtained the signed pedigree. This may be the pet name you call him at home, or it may be something considerably fancier. Many cats are named for a relative in their pedigree which they resemble. In order to do this, however, bear in mind that some associations require written permission from the owner of the cat you are naming after. Combinations of sire and dam names may be used. A cat's registered name, in itself, may tell a great deal about him.

If the breeder of your kitten has a cattery name, such as "Dearheart," it should precede his "given" name, comparable to a surname in reverse. If this is the case, you may, with the breeder's approval, give the kitten any name that has not already been used by the cattery. The only exception to this is that another registered cattery name, such as "Reene" or "Francine," may not be used as a "given" name. If you, too, have a cattery name, it may be added after the given name, if the total number of letters does not exceed the limit of approximately 27 letters, which is the average permitted. The limit varies among the associations.

Thus a name such as "Dearheart Bianca of Reene's" means that Bianca originally came from Dearheart cattery, but now is owned by Reene's cattery.

If the breeder has no cattery name, you must furnish three choices of name. Over the years, someone else may have used your first choice and it would be disallowed. If none of the three you choose is available, the association usually will suggest a variation of spelling that may be used.

Some breeders register all the kittens as a litter, at which time they may or may not register yours for you, by its individual name. If you are to take care of the name registration yourself, be sure you are given the signed litter registration slip for your kitten, in addition to the pedigree.

Cattery Names

A few suggestions to new breeders on the selection of a cattery name, by Mrs. Fannie Mood, retired C.F.A. Recorder, follow:

Care and thought should be used in selecting a cattery name. Since it is to be your trademark, it should be dignified, yet catchy, and easy to remember. It must not be more than 12 letters in length. Shorter is better, because the shorter it is, the more leeway you have for a cat's name, as the limit of letters allowed for a cat's name includes any cattery names. Try to select a name that has not been used extensively for cat names, since you would not want cats owned and bred by others to be carrying names similar to your cattery name. One way to make sure of this is to coin a word of your own. Perhaps a part of your own name or a combination of part of your name and part of your husband's, or a child's name. An example of this is the Mil-War (Mildred and Warren) Cattery. Another suggestion is your street or town name, if it is a pretty one and would fit in with other names.

How to Register

The Cat Fanciers' Association is the most popular registering organization. It has maintained continuous printed registration records, in the form of Studbooks, since 1909. Nearly 10,000 cats and kittens were registered with this organization during 1962.

If you have purchased the pedigree, the first step in applying for the registration of your cat is to obtain the official form of the association you choose, which may be obtained free from the association's office. Fees vary slightly, but the usual charge for registration is approximately $2.00.

A CFA registration number for your cat and their acceptance of his name will almost automatically insure his eligibility for subsequent registration either as an individual or as a parent in any one of the other associations. Therefore, the best procedure is to apply for your cat's registration with the CFA first.

The information requested on the form should be copied from the pedigree. You must furnish, also, three choices of name. Send both the form and the registration fee to the Recorder. This form is kept in the files, after it has been checked against the records for possible errors. If all is in order, your cat's name and identification number in that association are recorded. Your cat's exact formal name, once accepted, may not be changed, nor may it ever be used for any other cat. The association will mail you a certificate of registration listing all the necessary facts of your cat's identity. This is also the title of ownership, similar to the one issued for your automobile. A form is provided on the back for use in the event of sale of the cat. To become official, such transfers of ownership must be sent to the association for recording.

The registration number and name recorded for your cat apply *only* to the business of the association which issued it and for future pedigree information. In order to claim wins in shows, it is necessary your cat be registered in the sponsoring association. In some cases, such as C.F.A. shows, the registration number is required before the cat may be entered. Other associations allow a cat to be "listed," for a nominal fee, but require registration after points have been received toward Champion status.

18

BEAUTY OF DREAM HARBOR and two of her daughters. Photo by Hans Bomskow.

National Organizations:

The Cat Fanciers' Association, Inc.,

Mrs. Myrtle Shipe, *Secretary*,
20615 Patton Court,
Detroit 28, Michigan.
   Recorder
   River Hill Building,
   39 East Front Street,
   Red Bank, New Jersey.

The American Cat Association, Inc.,

Mrs. Stanley Gibson,
Secretary-Recorder,
Lakeside, Berrien County,
Michigan.

Cat Fanciers' Federation,

Richard Orman, *Secretary*,
409 South 22nd Street,
Philadelphia 46, Pennsylvania.
   Mrs. Florence Kanoffe, *Recorder*,
   Route 80,
   North Guilford, Connecticut.

American Cat Fanciers' Association,

Porter Walley, *Secretary*.
   Mrs Porter Walley, *Recorder*,
   1104 Bouldin Avenue,
   Austin 4, Texas.

United Cat Federation, Inc.,

Mrs. Barbara Layton, *Secretary*,
1321 Malena Drive,
Santa Ana, California.
   Miss Katherine Beswick, *Recorder*,
   P.O. Box 652,
   Cardiff-by-the-Sea, California.

National Cat Fanciers Association,
                              Inc.,

Mrs. Frances Kosierowski,
Secretary-Recorder,
8219 Rosemont Road,
Detroit 28, Michigan.

II

THE WORLD OF SHOW CATS

Cat Clubs

There are approximately 250 cat clubs in the United States today, formed by persons who have a common interest in cats. You may join one whether or not you own a cat. The clubs usually hold monthly meetings at which the welfare of cats in general and the problems of the members' cats in particular are discussed. The membership of an all-breed club is made up of persons who either own or are interested in cats of various breeds, as the name implies. There are also many specialty clubs for individual breeds of shorthairs and for the color groups of long-haired cats. Most of the local specialty clubs are CFA affiliates; some non-affiliated societies for the furtherance of specific colors and kinds of cats have nationwide membership.

Members of a cat club plan and put on cat shows which are conducted under the rules of the association with which the club is affiliated. Judges are selected from those approved by the association. If you are interested in attending a show either as an exhibitor or spectator, you can find out when one is to be held near your home from the secretaries of the national organizations or from the show schedule in *CATS MAGAZINE*. The secretaries also can put you in touch with your local cat club, should you be interested in joining one or receiving entry blanks to exhibit.

Show Entries

The show season for long-haired cats starts in the early fall and runs through the winter until late spring. From November through February, most of the longhairs are in their best coats, so shows are held nearly every weekend during that period. The shows usually are two-day affairs, starting Saturday morning and

A view of a cat show. Seating area for spectators, trophy display, and judging area are in foreground. Rows of exhibit cages where cats are on display are separate, at background. Photo by Hans Bomskow.

ending Sunday night. If you enter your cat, it is required that he be present the entire time. You may take him home with you overnight or leave him in his cage in the showroom, as you prefer.

Entries are solicited by the club approximately two months ahead of the date of the show. The entry list is closed three or four weeks before show date. Entry information supplied by the club's entry clerk states the date, time, and place of show, prizes to be given, names of officiating judges, size of exhibit display cages provided, and other information pertinent to the conduct of the show.

Usually a Longhair and a Shorthair Specialty Show, and sometimes shows for groups of shorthair breeds or longhair colors, are held in conjunction with an All-Breed Show, each having its own judge. You must enter the All-Breed; you may enter the appropriate Specialty Show, too. Entry fees are approximately $3.00 for each All-Breed, and $2.50 for each Specialty.

Return to the clerk the completed entry blank, together with fees, before the closing date. Be sure to enter your cat's name and other information concerning him *exactly* as appear on his registration certificate. Your wins may be voided if the information you furnish is not correct. If your cat is not registered, he may be "listed," as explained in the section "How to Register."

Show Classifications

The non-championship classes include Kittens, purebreds from four to eight months of age; A.O.C., Any-Other-Color purebred cats which do not conform to the recognized color requirements; and Household Pets, cats and kittens of unknown or mixed ancestry. Championship classes for older, unaltered, purebred cats are Novice, Open, Champion, and Grand Champion. The Novice is for only those cats over eight months of age (in some associations, not over two years) which have not yet won a First ribbon, or, in some cases, "winner's points." The Open in-includes all cats which have not won the required number of points to claim championship. Champion and Grand Champion classes are for those who have achieved that status. There are corresponding classes for altered cats, i.e., neuters (males) and spays (females), called Premiership, or Peerless.

Show Catalogue

Entries are classified according to breed, color, sex, and classes. An official printed catalogue is available at the show, giving age, parentage, and ownership of each cat entered. Each is given his catalogue number for that show. Usually an acknowledgment of your entry's acceptance is sent. The closing of the entries a month ahead of time enables the show's management to make all the necessary arrangements. It is rather difficult, however, for the exhibitor to guess in what condition the coat of his cat may be, that far ahead of time. Quite often, the one you did *not* enter is the one that might have won, and the one you *did* enter should have stayed home.

When You Arrive . . .

When you arrive at the show, your cat is examined by a veterinarian, usually before you are permitted to bring him into the showroom. This is a protection for both your cat and those of other exhibitors. If he appears to be in good health, you are assigned to a display cage provided by the management. You "furnish" the interior to your own taste in the way of draperies, floor covering, and so on, to best show off your exhibit. Sanitary litter and food usually are provided, but you bring your own container and dishes.

Judging Procedure

Judging cages are in a separate enclosure and are undecorated. The judge has no knowledge of your cat other than the catalogue number listed under his designated class. When this number is placed on top of one of the judging cages by the clerk, the cat then is "called" for judging. Show etiquette prescribes that you place your cat, when "called," *promptly* into the designated judging cage from the rear, if possible, to preserve his anonymity. Be sure front door is closed! Novice males of a color are called first. The order of the colors may be changed, but usually is as it appears in the catalogue. Owners and other spectators may watch the judging procedure from seats provided in front of the judging area. Any questions or corrections you may have regarding your cat must be handled through the clerk.

The judge removes the cat from the front of the cage and places him on the table to be checked for his conformation to the official standard. The clerk may be asked the age of the cat. In order for a cat to compete for any award, the rules require that the judge must at least place a hand on the cat. If a cat seems unwilling to let the judge handle him, the owner may be called to assist. This does not count against the cat in the judging, but a judge, naturally, is better able to appreciate the cat's fine points if he is well behaved. Each cat is gone over individually by the judge and then compared with the others in the same class. The first awarding of ribbons is then made.

Ribbons

A blue ribbon hung on his cage indicates the cat that has won first place in his class. A red ribbon is for second, yellow for third, and green, fourth. The other cats of the same color and sex then are judged in their respective classes, and ribbons hung. The winning cat in the Male Novice class is compared with the winning cat of the Male Open class, in competition for "winner's points." This winner is awarded another ribbon—usually striped red, white, and blue, or solid purple, which indicates points toward Champion status. At least three sets of such ribbons must be won from different judges to complete a cat's championship. A reserve winner also is chosen, in case the winner should be disqualified. The same procedure applies for female cats.

Grand Champions

In some associations, the Champion classes are designated as Junior and Senior, and the blue-ribbon champions from each compete for Champion Winner's points toward Grand Champion status. However, there are additional requirements to be met which are comparable to the procedure followed by the other associations for the title of Grand Champion.

The specific requirements vary in each association. The meaning and quality of this title may be summarized by defining a Grand Champion as a "champion of champions." A cat who is a Grand Champion has more than once been adjudged Best Champion (or Best Opposite Sex Champion) over other champions of different colors and kinds.

Best of Color

Best of Sex is chosen next, from the "Winner's Cat," the First-Place Champion, and First-Place Grand Champion. No ribbon is awarded at this time. The female cats of the same color are then judged in the same manner as the males.

The Best Male and Best Female are compared for Best of Color. The better of the two receives a ribbon or rosette reading "Best of Color"; the other is awarded one reading "Best Opposite Sex." Neither ribbon means, necessarily, that that cat's color is the best possible; it means only that, overall, it is the best cat of that color in the show.

Best Opposite Sex

"Best" is an easily comprehended designation for a win; however, "Best Opposite Sex" seems to create some confusion in the mind of the novice exhibitor and spectator, especially the shortened "Best Opposite" used conversationally. If the cat judged Best of Color, Division, Class, or In Show is a male, then a female is "Best Opposite Sex." Conversely, when a female is judged Best, a male is "Best Opposite Sex." This often is abbreviated "B.O.X." or "B.X."

Kittens, Household Pets, and Altered Cats are judged separately, in a similar manner, and Bests awarded. They do not compete with other cats for Best In Show, etc.

Top Awards

This same procedure is followed for each color. Divisional, or color group, preliminary Bests are chosen from these Best of Colors and Opposites. Then, in All-Breed Shows, Best and Opposite Longhair, Best and Opposite Shorthair, and finally Best in Show, Second Best, Best Opposite Sex, and Second Best Opposite Sex are chosen. Rosettes and, usually, trophies or other prizes are given. Specialty Shows are for either Longhairs or Shorthairs, so the preceding first two wins are not awarded. All other wins are the same.

In addition, wins are given for Best and Best Opposite Sex In Show of each class—Novice, Open, Champion, and Grand Champion. Appropriately lettered rosettes, and sometimes trophies, are awarded for each of these wins. They are referred to as the "finals," or "top show," awards.

To be eligible to win the Best Cat In Show award, a cat must have been designated the best in each and every preliminary classification in which he competed. As these are completed, by the process of elimination it will become apparent which individual or individuals remain eligible.

Second Best Cat In Show must have been defeated by *only* one cat, the Best Cat In Show, anywhere along the line. Thus it is possible for a cat which received a red, or second, ribbon to the Best Cat's blue, or first, in their very first judging of color classes, to be eligible for Second Best Cat In Show. This rarely, if ever, happens.

Your cat may be eligible for one of the class Bests, even though he has received nothing further than a blue ribbon in his own class, so do not take him home without first determining whether or not he could be called up in the finals, as cats, nearly always, must be present in order to receive any award.

Win or Lose

In the Specialty Shows, cats are judged by a different judge, following the same procedures. Your cat competes against the same cats as in the All-Breed; otherwise, the Show awards are entirely separate—and sometimes different. Thus apparent reversals are quite possible, due to the fact that many very good

"First" and "Winners" ribbons bring thrill to owner Patti O'Hearn.

specimens are competing, none perfect. The faults and good features may be different, but the overall point score is nearly the same. Many decisions are very close. If your cat is a loser, hope for better luck next time.

To the novice exhibitor, the showing of his cat can be an exciting experience. As a matter of fact, those who are *not* novices find each showing of their cats an exciting experience, regardless of how many times they have done it before.

As a novice, the wins your cat receives will give you an idea of how his qualities compare with those of other cats; however, the rating he makes at any one show depends, in part, on the competition that is present. You cannot begin to come to a true conclusion about his show potential until you have tried him in several shows, and against a variety of competing cats.

Many persons feel that they themselves are being judged instead of their cats. This is an attitude to guard against. Bear in mind, too, that your cat's feelings are neither hurt nor helped by the award he gets, even though yours are.

When your cat loses, learn to hide your disappointment so as not to spoil the other fellow's pleasure in his win. There is always some good feature of the competitor's cat you can admire. "Do unto others . . ." applies to the owners of winners as well as to owners of losers at a cat show.

Spectator Etiquette

Most exhibitors are glad to show off their cats and answer questions about them. If the cats are back in their display cages and are not being made ready for the judges, their owners are usually available to talk to. However, do not touch anyone's cat without permission. Not only could you possibly transmit disease by petting one cat and then another, but some cats are rather nervous at a show. Especially are you likely to upset both a cat and his owner if you reach toward them while they are en route to or from the judging area.

Cat shows are open for the general public to attend as spectators. Admission is charged. Each show draws from 125 to 200 exhibitors, showing a total of from 175 to 350 cats.

The Cream of the Crop

Since 1947, *Cats Magazine* has awarded "All American" honors to the top-winning show cats. These annual awards are based on counting the total number of other cats the contestant has defeated in all the shows in which he competed during that season. This includes shows sponsored by every association of cat fanciers, so this award is different from the titles and awards earned only within the associations themselves. Some of the associations also have Intra-Association awards similar to the "All American."

All-American Cats

Your cat as a contestant for an All-American award is scored as follows: each show in which he is exhibited during the show season, extending from May to the following May, is analyzed and scored by *Cats Magazine*. He earns one "color point" for each cat he has defeated in competition for Best of Color and one "class point" for each class included in whatever higher awards of Best he receives, such as Best of Division or Best Novice. His Best of Opposite Sex (color and class) wins are totaled in the same manner, except that only cats of the same sex as the contestant are counted.

A cat which has received a Best Cat in Show award, therefore, earns his color points (one for each cat of his same color), plus one class point for each and every class represented in that show. Second Best Cat in Show receives his own (different) color points, plus a proportion (85%, at the present time) of the class points won by the Best Cat. Best Opposite Sex Cat in Show receives his or her own (different) color points and one class point for each class of cats of his or her same sex in show. Kittens and Altered Cats are scored similarly, but their eligibility for a count to be run begins only when they receive a Best or Best Opposite Sex in Show award.

Annual awards are made to the highest scoring male and female in each of the color classes throughout all the varieties of show cats. First, they are computed and ribbons are sent on a Sectional, or geographical, basis: All-Western, All-Eastern, All-Southern, All-Midwestern, and All-Oceanic—for example, 1963

All-Western Black Persian Male. Then the highest scoring cat of these five preliminary winners is further awarded and designated 1963 All-American Black Persian Male. Rosettes are awarded to each of these All-American cats, kittens, and altered cats. The next highest scoring individuals are given Honorable Mention ribbons, in both the Sectional and the All-American awards competition.

The highest scoring of all the All-American cats is awarded the title "Cat of the Year." If this cat is a male, "Cat of the Year Opposite Sex" is given to the highest scoring of all the females, and vice versa. Most of the winners have been and some of these Persians have been Copper-Eyed Whites (CEW).

Following is a listing of the Cat of the Year award winners from 1975 back to 1958, as computed and published by Cats Magazine.

All-American Cats

1975 HAWTHORNE NITE LITER OF LEE. Black Persian male owned by Mr. and Mrs. William L. Lee.

1974 KALICO'S MARY POPPINS OF MARVONACK. Blue British Shorthair female owned by Jack and Yvonne Patrick.

1973 JOELWYN THE WILD ONE III OF NILE. Ruddy Abyssinian male owned by Marlene Nottingham.

1972 JOELWYN COLUMBYAN. Silver Tabby American Shorthair male owned by C. Raymond and Joann Sneed.

1971 LOWLAND'S ZEUS OF LIN-LEA. Cream Persian male owned by Ralph and Judy Beery.

1970 WALHALL'S ISOLDE. Black Persian female owned by Commander and Mrs. Alan H. Bath and Ted Napolski.

1969 CONALAN'S MISS PRETTEE OF WALHALL. Black Persian female owned by Commander and Mrs. Alan H. Bath and Ted Napolski.

1968 BURM-SI'S SIR HENRY. Sable Burmese male owned by William A. Carter.

1967 MIZPAH'S FERDNAND OF BRIERWOOD. Sable Burmese male owned by John Baker.

1966 PHAROH RAMSES II. Ruddy Abyssinian male owned by Bob and Kim Everett.

1965 SHAWNEE TRADEMARK. Silver Tabby American Shorthair male owned by Bill and Nikki Shuttleworth.

1964 SHAWNEE MOONFLIGHT. Copper-Eyed White Persian male owned by Bill and Nikki Shuttleworth.

1963 AZULITA PALEFACE OF CASA CIELO. Copper-Eyed White Persian male owned by Pat Johston.

1962 CHEZ MOUMETTE CAL OF NORMONT. Cream Persian male owned by Maurine Hoag.

1961 SHAWNEE MOONFLIGHT. Copper-Eyed White Persian male owned by Nikki Horner.

1960 SHAWNEE MOONFLIGHT. Copper-Eyed White Persian male owned by Nikki Horner.

1959 VEL-VENE'S VOODOO. Black Persian male owned by Robert A. Green.

1958 ROSEMONT GOLDEN BOY. Cream Persian male owned by Frances Kosierowski.

Keeping Up with the Cat World

Cats Magazine is the only magazine published in the United States that is strictly about cats. It contains articles on various phases of cat care, stories, poems, cat-book reviews, advertising of cats for sale, and cat products. Complete show information is given by listing all coming events, and, in later issues, the

Black male owned by Bess Morse: GR. CH. PIED PIPER OF BARBE BLEUE. CAT OF THE YEAR 1951. Sire: Dbl. Ch. Barbe Bleue Personality; dam: Barbe Bleue Mandy. Bred by Peggy Harbaugh.

record of show results and All-Sectional and All-American awards are published. It has nation-wide distribution on a subscription-only basis. A subscription order form can be obtained from secretaries of cat organizations and from breeders.

English Shows

The "fancying," or interest in the breeding and showing, of Persian cats has long been popular in England. The first cat show of note held anywhere in the world was in the Crystal Palace, London, in 1871. Harrison Weir, English artist, arranged the exhibition, at which many purebred Persians and Angoras were shown. Since the event proved successful, the first large cat show in the United States was held in a similar fashion, in Madison Square Garden, New York City, in 1895.

Over the years, American show procedures have diverged from the English type, as will be noted by the following brief summary of English procedures:

English judging is done by several judges, each covering one or more different classes, colors, or varieties. Each of these judges nominates one exhibit as his choice for Best in Show. These choices are examined by a panel of judges, sometimes an entirely different group. They then vote on the final choice by ballot.

Shows are usually one-day events. Entries are handled in the same general fashion as ours. A lapse of three weeks is desired between shows to avoid the possibility of contagion. On the morning of the show, after the veterinary inspection, the entrants are placed in unmarked exhibit cages. They are provided with numbered identity tags to be placed about their necks, and then left by their owners for the judges to examine.

The judges and stewards appointed by the show committee to handle the cats then proceed along the rows of undecorated and unmarked cages to evaluate the group of cats assigned to them. Slips are posted on the cages designating the awards given in the classes entered.

The classes are much more varied than those in the United States, and an exhibit may be entered in several classes. Awards are given for individuals in classes such as Kittens, Novices, and those not yet champions. These categories have slightly different requirements for age and prior wins than ours. Many cats that do not conform to the usual prescribed color requirements may be entered and shown as Any Other Color (A.O.C.). This is not a popular class in the United States. Monorchid males cannot be shown there; they may be shown here, with no penalty. There are classes for groups of cats and kittens, too. These are: Litter; Stud Cat or Brood Queen (judged by self and progeny); Brace or Team (two or several belonging to same owner); Club (for members only); and Breeders (those bred by owners), to list a few. English shows also have an Any Other Variety (A.O.V.) class.

A cat that has won three "Challenge Certificates," awarded in a fashion comparable to our "Winner's Points," is then a Champion. Only then may he be exhibited in other countries to compete for the title of International Champion, highest award possible to attain.

Only after the judging is entirely completed are the owners and visitors permitted to enter the area where the cats are caged.

Show Standards — English vs. American

Some differences are to be found in the standards of the one and only English association, the Governing Council of Cat Fanciers, or G.C.C.F. Following are the chief differences pertaining to the longhairs: a higher proportion of their total points is allotted to color alone; Peke-Face varieties are not recognized; there are no color classes for Shaded Silvers, one of our largest groups; only Chinchilla Silvers are accepted for showing; Odd-Eyed Whites are not eligible to be shown; Blue Creams should have their colors intermingled, rather than patched; and Himalayans are called Colour Point Longhairs.

There are some other varieties of longhairs in England which are virtually unknown here, such as the Burman, a type of longhair Siamese with white toes, and the Van (imported from Turkey), basically white with auburn head, back, and tail markings.

Blue and Chinchilla are the most popular longhair colors in England. Most of the American Persian stock of all colors were originally imported from there. Cats with individual excellence and good breeding potential are continually imported from England and Europe to be mixed with families of stock we have developed here. These cats are designated "Imported" (Imp.), along with their names, after they arrive here. Some of our cats have been imported by breeders in other countries, but the six-month quarantine imposed by England discourages most English breeders from importing cats.

Cat Fancy International

There are cat shows and fanciers all over the world. They are active in Canada, Australia, New Zealand, Japan, Denmark, Holland, France, Germany, and Switzerland, as well as in England and the United States. Federation Internationale Feline d'Europe, or F.I.F.E., is an association of European cat clubs that has many affiliates. Recently the way was made clear for an interchange of F.I.F.E. judges with C.F.A. judges.

Our Cats, a magazine exclusively about cats, is published in London, England. It is also subscribed to, and popular, here. It features views and news of the international cat scene.

III

CAT TRAITS AND TRICKS

Cats and Other Cats

Cats have interesting games that they play only with other cats. They have very tender relationships with each other that are a delight to observe. All of our cats gather around to comfort or come to the rescue of any one of the others who seems to be in distress. They wash one another's faces, ears, and other hard-to-reach places. An industrious female with strong washing instincts can keep everyone's fur slicked up and neat.

Our fifteen-year-old "grandma kitty," Itty Bitty, keeps law and order in our house. Any cat or kitten who is growling or seems to be causing a commotion is soundly swatted and put in his place by our "grandma."

Older cats will teach kittens how to behave properly. Two cats will keep each other company when you are not around, but they are seldom so attached to each other that they won't require their personal relationship with you, also, to round out their lives.

Cats and People

Each cat has a different personality. It is surprising how quickly these differences show up in a litter of kittens. Even before their eyes open, individual characteristics are noticed. Some are what we call "people cats." They particularly like human companionship. They will purr and try to rub their bodies against your hand, even before they can walk with any assurance. This type of responsiveness is a trait that seems to run in certain cat families.

Some are inclined toward conversation. This includes "talking" to themselves as well as to you. There are many tones to a cat's voice. Although you may not understand exactly what is being said you usually will get the idea.

Shaded Silver male owned by Dr. and Mrs. P. N. Ramsdale: TR. CH. SIR ANTHONY DEARHEART. Sire: Mi Ti of Rol-ing Hills; dam: Princess Belita. Bred by Edith Vaughan. Photo by Gordon Laughner.

One of our males, Sir Anthony Dearheart, "talked" only to my husband. "Tony" would wait for his homecoming and then proceed earnestly to tell him of all the happenings of the day. The final sentence was undoubtedly "and I haven't had a bite to eat since you left." (This, of course, was not true.) He would then usher my sympathetic spouse to the kitchen to receive a handout from him. It was just the personal contact he wanted, as often no more would be done for him than to stir around the food I had already provided. This food then, apparently, would taste entirely different, and he would polish off the plate. This was a daily routine.

This particular cat, now deceased, had many traits that appear to be inherited by his progeny. He always slept upside down, stretched out full-length on his back, paws folded on his chest. He did not care to sit on laps, but enjoyed being carried on the shoulder to see how the house looked from a different level. He liked to eat bread and cake. He was easily offended if you laughed at him. He sulked to the extent of turning his head away when he had to walk by you, or if you tried to make up before he was ready to do so.

Personality Differences

A few of our cats retrieve paper wads or balls thrown to them. One of my females, Beauty, who has this characteristic, will keep on and on with it, long after you are tired of the game. If I remove her toy, she will get a piece of paper out of the wastebasket and bring it to me.

Other cats use their paws like hands. It is amusing to watch one eat his food by fishing it out of the plate and carrying it up to his mouth with a paw. Females of this type handle their kittens with their paws, instead of carrying them in their mouths.

Many cats sit up on their haunches like rabbits to get a better look at something that interests them. Some will sit up that way for quite a while, stretching their necks up higher from time to time. I particularly like that pose as seen from the rear.

All cats like to pretend, and many of their elaborate games and play routines show great imagination.

Some Persians like to sit on your lap. Most of them do not like to do so, nor to be held. They probably become too hot, or you may accidentally pull their hair when you handle them. However, they will sit or lie near you, and wherever you may be in the house they all usually soon join you.

Some Persians seem to prefer men; others like women better. Some prefer children to adults. If there is more than one person in your home, you may need to have more than one cat to go around.

Discipline

Cats seem to be impressed by noise and commotion. Sharp clapping of hands and loud noises with paper will at least make a cat pause in the course of wrong-doing. Try to make it appear that the interesting forbidden object—such as the bird, rug, furniture, or door—is itself attacking him with a noise.

They can learn "No!"—but do not always wish to admit it. They do respond to praise and love and, in general, want to please you. All cats are much like small children and will do anything to get your attention, even by actions they know will be frowned upon. In like manner, undesirable conduct is used to express displeasure at your treatment—such as leaving a cat home all alone or scolding him.

Cats and Other Pets

An older cat will usually accept a kitten. There may be growling and spitting at first, if the little one presumes to get too close. Kittens want to be friendly with other cats, but they have sense enough to "freeze" and retreat if they are rebuffed. After a while, though, the older one will rather enjoy watching the antics of a baby and forget dignity and join in the fun.

Most Persians get along with and like, or at least tolerate, most dogs and other pets. They are more favorably inclined toward the less noisy dogs, those that do not have a shrill bark. It is best to introduce strangers to one another gradually. Always be with them, at first. By the time the new pet has acquired a familiar "house smell," you can leave him alone with another animal, assuming no violent hostility has manifested itself.

There may be a great deal of jealousy at first. You can help this situation by giving extra attention and reassurance to the jealous one. He blames you more than the interloper for the change in his household, anyway. He may punish you with "mistakes" or by refusing food for a while.

Cats and Infants

The old wives' tale that a cat will suck a baby's breath, thereby killing it, continues to be passed from generation to generation as an alleged fact. It is time that a plea was entered for a reasonable evaluation of the probabilities and possibilities of the truth of such a statement.

I have heard tales about this many times, but never from anyone who could claim having witnessed such a procedure. It has always been third-hand—someone's neighbor was told by someone else that it happened to someone she knew, and the like. I have often wondered just how (or why) it was accomplished, if indeed it were. The mouth of a cat is not designed to "suck" air, food, or milk. Nor have I ever seen a cat past nursing-kitten age ever do so for any reason. *Have you?* The lung capacity of a cat is considerably less than that of a baby, which, in itself, further bears out the physical impossibility of the act.

Our cats were greatly concerned whenever either of our children was crying in actual distress. They would become quite agitated if the crying continued, go look in the crib, then come after me to insist I *do* something, but a baby's crying that was strictly for attention was ignored.

A cat's extra-sensory awareness of danger, plus his acute sense of hearing and extreme curiosity, conceivably could combine to send him to the crib to investigate a baby's distress. He might be found licking a baby's face—but in an attempt to revive it. He might be trying to warm it back to life with his body as instinctively as he would do for another cat, thus giving rise to erroneous conclusions based upon misunderstanding of the circumstances.

Fear that a beloved pet cat will automatically turn into a demon upon the advent of a new baby in the household is completely unfounded in fact. It is most unfortunate that such a fallacy has been permitted to persist and cause otherwise reasonable persons to give away their cats or have them destroyed before considering whether it is likely—or *possible*—that a cat will "suck the baby's breath"!

Cat Tales

There are as many tales of interesting cats, their actions and reactions, as there have been individual cats and persons to observe them. Each cat and each tale adds yet another plane to the multi-faceted enjoyment you can derive from living with a cat. When telling what your cat does, you are likely to have your best tale interrupted by someone else who is eager to relate what *his* cat does. Your only defense is to write a book of cat tales yourself.

IV

THE RIGHT KITTEN

All Kittens Become Cats

When you acquire a kitten, you are also acquiring a grown cat. The cute ways of all kittens are most attractive; however, in a year or so, your kitten will grow up, and the kind of adult he will be depends on his inherited qualities and tendencies, as well as the "bringing up" you give him.

Most Persian kittens sold are the result of planned breeding. This is a great advantage to the buyer. Cat nature being what it is, some very unsuitable matches would occur if matings were not planned. When you purchase a purebred kitten, whether you buy the papers or not, you have the assurance that a great deal of thought and work have gone into making your kitten what it is. Personality traits, good health, and beauty of form and coat are not accidental. Your kitten's pedigree is the record of how all these things have been blended for at least four generations.

A cattery owner or breeder knows what kind of grown cat your kitten is likely to be, because he knows the qualities of its grown-up relatives. The tracing of the kitten's lineage is important, even if you don't plan to show or breed your Persian. The ancestry will give you some idea of its inherited disposition and potential quality, and it is proof that it is purebred.

All Cats Are Pets

Many people wish their cats to be just a beautiful pet. They have no desire to show their cats in competition or to raise kittens. Of course, all cats are potential pets. Any cat, whether kept strictly as a pet or to be bred or shown, responds to human attention. A cat or kitten that has the benefit of the extra individual attention bestowed on it by its human "family" stands a better chance of developing its full potential character.

Quality and Price

In evaluating them for sale, most Persian kittens may be placed in one of three general categories: pet-quality, possible show-type, and those with definite show potential. A pet-quality kitten should cost about $50.00. The price may be somewhat less, if enteritis vaccination has not been given, or if pedigree papers are not included. If you do not purchase the pedigree of the kitten, be sure to have it clearly understood, preferably in writing, that papers are available and at what additional cost, should you want them later. In addition, if he has been inoculated, get a certificate to that effect. You will find more information about papers and the necessity for enteritis vaccination elsewhere in this book.

If you are considering the possibility of breeding or showing a Persian, acquaint yourself with the standard, and, if possible, attend a cat show before making your purchase. Then go to a breeder of experience and good reputation and rely on his judgment as to which kitten to purchase.

Small imperfections in coat color or markings are often the factors determining the sale price. The standards given for the fine points of the various colors may be used as a guide to a kitten's possibilities as a show cat. Small variations from the desired quality are of no consequence, *if he is not going to compete at a show;* if he is, these fine points are of prime importance.

The difference between the pet and show types often is apparent only to the trained eye. No breeder wants cats from his cattery to be shown unless they are potential winners. Show kittens or cats, of course, will cost more. It is well worth the initial investment if you do plan to breed or show them.

Before Adoption

A strong sturdy body, apparent good health, and intelligence are important to anyone buying a kitten, regardless of what price is paid.

Be sure the kitten you choose is alert, with bright and clear eyes. He should be well fleshed, with a substantial feel. These are characteristics of the healthy Persian. Steer clear of a kitten with a runny nose, sore ears, skin lesions, or drab-looking, harsh-feeling coat. It is a wise precaution to have the kitten checked by a veterinarian for less obvious conditions. A "bargain-price" animal can cost a great deal more in disappointment and veterinary care than one purchased at the usual price. Wait a little, and save for the right one if you cannot afford it now, or make a deposit so the breeder will reserve one for you.

A Persian kitten should be at least nine to ten weeks of age before he is taken to a new home. The extra weeks with his mother after weaning provide a much better start in life; further, the kitten has had time to receive its two feline enteritis vaccinations at eight and nine weeks, and to build up his immunity to this common, dangerous, and nearly always fatal disease. His digestive processes have developed sufficiently by this age so that a change in environment, food, and water will not make him sick. Further, more of his individual personality pattern is apparent, and his mother has had time to teach him some of the ways of life.

Boy or Girl?

Unless you have have a particular reason for requiring that your new pet be of a certain sex, choose your kitten on the basis of its own personality. If an individual kitten appeals strongly to you, it is more likely to be the right one for you.

After you have chosen your kitten, or it has chosen you, be prepared to enjoy its development from babyhood through adolescence to full flower as an adult. Females generally mature to their full beauty at two to three years of age. Males of four or five years of age are at their peak. The older they become, the more personality, intelligence, and beauty they possess, so that your ownership is a continuing pleasure.

The following chapters will help you better to understand a cat's nature. Then you can apply common-sense measures to avoid or cope with problems that may arise.

V

HE, SHE, OR IT

How Will Altering Affect a Cat?

The sex-altering operation for the male is called *neutering*; for the female, it is known as *spaying*. When either is performed, the mating urge is changed, or neutralized, so that, in the male, it no longer is the cat's main objective in life. The other facets of an altered cat's nature then have a chance to come to the fore, and interest in things other than sex life develop. Altered cats are more playful and more interested in people as the focal point of their lives. This is what most of us desire in a pet cat, and altering is one of the best ways to help obtain it.

Another benefit of altering is that long-haired cats of either sex are more likely to hold a better coat of fur all year round. If unaltered, a long-haired cat is subject to extreme shedding of coat in the spring to "strip down" for the mating game. After having been altered, they shed the old coat to some extent, but not as freely, and the ruff area does not get bare.

Cats do not have to have the experience of motherhood or fatherhood before being altered. A cat's sexual urges are instinctive, but they are stimulated by the sex hormones in the body. If this stimulus is removed before a sex-behavior pattern has been set by practice, there is no frustration set up.

Even in a young male cat it will take a few weeks, perhaps months, for the full effect of altering to be realized, especially if it is performed after sex urges have developed. Eight to ten months is the recommended age for neutering males, as by this time the adolescent cat has reached sufficient bodily development for the operation not to affect his growth. On the other hand, he has not quite reached the age where the habits of sexual gratification have been set, which would need to be forgotten.

Particularly, do not look for an instant change in the case of an older male. It may take a little more time for the good results to become apparent. Even though some of the old actions might remain as habit reflexes, at least there will be an improvement, as the fuel for the fire no longer will be present. Allow time for the hormone balance of his system to change.

An altered male or female cat does not automatically become fat and lazy. The only thing that happens to a cat's nature following alteration is that which has to do with the urge to mate.

Tom-Cat Behavior

A normal mature male usually has his mind on the probabilities of someone wishing to receive his loving attentions. Many show no discretion as to suitability, pursuing very young kittens and other males as well as possibly willing and able females.

The sex drive of a cat is a very powerful urge and is foremost in the minds of most male cats at all times. He is restless in the house and yowls at windows and doors to be let out and roam. He feels he might just run across a female somewhere if he scouts around. In the course of this pursuit he is likely to meet other males with the same thought. If he does, battle will ensue between them to eliminate possible competition for the female's favors. Moreover, with his mind on finding a mate, the male is likely to roam too far from home and become lost. He may not be careful about crossing streets, thereby risking being struck by a car.

Many male cats, if kept in, will "spray," wetting on or in any handy (for him) place in the house. This is to advertise to other cats, females especially, that he is present, available, and willing.

Not all male cats find it necessary to spray. This does not mean they have any less sexual power than those that do. If your male does not, you are fortunate. He either doesn't want to or he hasn't thought of it yet.

Neutering

Ordinarily, the neutering of a male by a veterinarian is a short, simple operation, done under an anesthetic. Seldom is there any pain or discomfort, nor do complications result after surgery. It usually involves only an overnight stay at the hospital, at most.

Cost of neutering a male generally is less than $10.00, but

should added surgical work be necessary, it would involve a small extra charge, plus a little longer hospitalization.

Problems Peculiar to Males

Monorchidism describes the condition of a male with only one of the two testicles visible. Occasionally, both testicles are retained, or invisible; this is called cryptorchidism.

In the normal long-haired males the testicles, or sperm-producing organs of the male cat, usually drop into their proper position in the scrotum at birth, or at least by eight months of age. If one testicle is retained in the abdominal cavity, that male is only half as potent for fertilizing the female's ova as one who has the usual working two. The inside temperature of the body is too high for producing live sperm cells.

Sometimes the urge to mate is not as strong in the monorchid cat, yet at other times it seems to make little difference in either his fertility or his desire. A male having both testicles inside would, naturally, be unable to produce live sperm cells. He very well could have the same desire to mate as any other male.

It is not known whether or not monorchidism is always an inherited tendency. It may be due to faulty development in any individual male cat. Hormone injections may be given, which sometimes bring the retained testicle down into proper position. Chances of success, however, are poor.

The disadvantage of breeding to a male with this tendency, if it proves to be inherited, shows up when his male kittens are to be neutered. The neutering process for a monorchid is considerably more than the usual minor operation. It consists of cutting and tying-off the cord between each of the testicles and the body, plus removal of the testicles themselves. It is more of a surgical risk to find the missing testicle, which may be only a little way inside the abdomen or a long way inside.

It is essential that both testicles be removed for the altering to be effective. If the one inside is allowed to remain there, it continues to secrete the hormones that give the male the urge to mate. No kittens could result, but the urge to mate would remain.

The purpose of altering a male is to destroy the mating urge as well as to sterilize or render him incapable of fathering kittens. If only sterilization is accomplished, the altering serves little purpose.

If a male is mated to a "proven" female (one which has had kittens before) but no kittens result, male-hormone treatment may be tried. This, possibly, would induce the production of more sperm, or sperm with more pep and life, to do the job.

Hormone treatment may also be given to a grown male to increase his urge to mate, if he is lacking in desire.

Behavior of a Female in Season

Female cats in season will "call" and chirp. A female will use varying tones and degrees of loudness to let it be known she would like a mate. Some females are more demonstrative than others at this time. They rub on everything and roll over and over on the floor. If a female is naturally very loving, it is difficult sometimes for you to tell when she is in season. If you are in doubt, run your hand down her back to the base of her tail. She will crouch down, work her hind feet, and curl her tail over to one side. Some females, when in season, will "spray" like a male, or wet anywhere.

Spaying

As a female's mating urge is seasonal, the age at which she is spayed is not as important as it is in the male. Results are much the same at whatever age the operation is performed. Have your female spayed at an early age if you do not intend to have any kittens. The most advantageous time is between six and eight months of age, after she has cut her permanent teeth and before she has been seriously in season. If the cat is permitted to go outdoors, have her spayed before six months of age; otherwise, she quite likely will become pregnant.

If you do not wish to have any *more* kittens, have your female spayed a week or so after she goes out of season, or as soon as her milk glands have dried up after the kittens are weaned.

The entire inside sexual apparatus of a female should be completely removed. This is done, under anesthetic, by making an incision in the abdomen and removing the uterus and ovaries. Stitches hold the incision together until all the muscles and layers of skin that have been cut through have started to heal. The skin stitches are generally removed by the doctor after about a week, when she receives her check-up. The cost ranges from $20.00 to $25.00 for a young female. Hospitalization time varies from overnight to several days, according to your veterinarian's usual practice.

To spay a female who is in season may cost a little more, and there is more risk involved. The organs have an increased blood supply at this time. Also, it is sometimes desirable, or necessary, to spay a female who is already pregnant. The risk of added shock is in proportion to the amount of mass removed. The sooner the better in the case of spaying the pregnant female.

For the same reason, it is not generally recommended to spay a female at the same time that she must undergo a Caesarian. This, however, is a decision for your veterinarian to make. At the time the question arises, circumstances may be such that it is a necessary step. Such circumstances could be the discovery of a severe infection or damage to the uterus.

Unfortunately, there are cases where a cat of any age or sex has a bad reaction to an anesthetic. Death from this cause is comparatively rare, but can happen sometimes even before any actual surgery is done, if the cat is allergic to any anesthetic, or to the particular one that is being used. This is something that cannot be predicted. All possible measures are taken in modern veterinary hospitals to protect your cat's life before, during, and after surgery.

VI

THE MATING GAME

There seem to be quite a few incorrect popular ideas about cats' sex lives, mating processes, and the having of kittens. The following should help explain and clarify these misconceptions.

Frequency of "Season"

A female cat can and does come in "season," or "heat," at varying intervals. Some female kittens come in season as early as four to five months of age and are capable of becoming pregnant that young. As pregnancy is very hard on a female kitten who is herself a baby at less than a year of age, take precautions to see that this does not happen.

The time lapse between one "season" and another is also variable. Some cats have an interval of three to four weeks between seasons. Others are out of season only a few days before they are in again. In the late winter and early spring nearly every female cat will come in season. She will continue to do so, on her own time schedules, until she is bred. Usually, though not always, there is a short lull in the cycles during the summer, which can start up again in the fall, but with less frequency.

Some cats follow a predictable pattern; others do not. A cat who has just had kittens and is nursing them can, and often does, come in season and get pregnant again immediately. This is most unfortunate, of course. A mother cat will nearly always come in season sometime between a few days after giving birth and the time the kittens are eight weeks old.

In other words, your female cat can come in season and be bred, with or without your permission, *at any time.*

The ova, or eggs, of a female cat are not present waiting to be fertilized by the male sperm, as is the case in many other animals —ovulation is induced by the sexual act itself. Incidentally, the size of the litter is dependent primarily on the number of eggs that the female produces to be fertilized at that time.

The only time the sire would have any effect on the size of a litter would be if just a few of his sperm were strong enough to fertilize; this, naturally, is rather uncommon. As is the case with humans, the determination of the sex of the offspring is a matter of chance, depending on the sperm.

Very few cases of double-mating and the conception of kittens from more than one male occur; however, it is entirely possible for this to happen. Do not let your female get out to possibly breed again with another male after she has been mated to the desired sire. Females do not always go out of season as soon as they are bred and have conceived. They often remain in the mood to be wooed for several days.

A common mistaken notion, ridiculous if you stop to think about it, is that if a purebred cat (or other animal) mates with another variety she is ruined for future breeding. One family of babies, by whatever kind of father, would have no bearing on any future families. There is no connection, any more than there is in human beings.

Mating Your Female

Many young Persian males, though they are willing, are not too adept at lovemaking. They all seem to know the first step, which is to hold the female by the nape of her neck. Further than that, it seems to be a trial-and-error process until they catch on to the proper way.

The proper way does involve quite a little cooperation on the part of the female, so it is best to mate the young males to experienced females. Similarly, customary procedure is to try a young female with an experienced and proven-to-be-fertile male.

Best source for obtaining a male to breed your female is a reputable breeder. Contact him ahead of time to arrange the details. Many require a veterinarian's certificate of health before accepting a female for breeding. This is to protect your female from disease as much as possible, as well as to protect the male.

Several attempts, at different times, may be necessary to breed a young female, even by a proven male. Have it understood at the beginning whether there will be an extra charge for more than one service. The charge for breeding is called a stud fee; it is payable in advance.

Sometimes a breeder will be willing (even eager) to accept "choice of litter" instead of payment of stud fee; if so, unless otherwise agreed upon beforehand, his kitten shall be his undisputed choice of the litter. Further, it is his prerogative to choose the male he wishes to be the sire. A breeder seldom, if ever, will want a kitten from an unregistered mother.

Even if a stud fee is paid, the breeder will want to know your female's parentage in order to advise the best choice of mate. He will want the ensuing kittens to be a credit to him, too, through their sire.

Breeding Persian kittens is a specialized field. It should not be undertaken by a novice without careful consideration of what would be involved in time, effort, and adequate facilities for the care and sale of the prospective family. If you do want your female to have a litter of kittens, maintaining close contact with an experienced breeder and with your veterinarian through all the phases will prevent costly errors.

Your breeder can help you select the best mate for your female and give you valuable advice about family traits. The mating should be planned and arranged for in advance of the actual breeding time.

It is well to bring the female to the male at the first sign of real "calling" or "rolling." The trip and strange surroundings often will put lovemaking out of her mind on arrival. This is particularly true in the case of a pet cat. Then, after a day or so of settling down, the urge will reassert itself and she will be agreeable to mating.

VII

THE EXPECTANT MOTHER

Symptoms of Pregnancy

There are no outward physical signs of pregnancy in the female cat until about three to four weeks after breeding. At that time, occasionally sooner, her nipples become a darker, brighter pink and begin to enlarge. There is a feeling of fullness in the lower rib area.

Pregnancy in the cat can be verified by an experienced veterinarian as early as three weeks from the time of breeding. In fact, from three to four weeks is the ideal time to check. At this point, the veterinarian can feel the uterus, which is naturally more enlarged, and often can count the number of kittens as lumps the size of ping-pong balls. These are not to be confused with the cat's kidneys, which are much the same size and shape. Knowing approximately how many kittens to expect is useful at the time of delivery.

By the time the cat is five or six weeks pregnant, the kittens are getting to a size that can be noticed as lumps. From this time on, the female will become larger and her appetite will increase.

From the moment they are bred, some females show many symptoms that are more usual later in pregnancy. They have a ravenous appetite, sleep most of the time, and make "nests" all over the house. Pregnancy makes some cats feel very cross; others are extra loving and sweet. Once in a while, in the early stages, they are afflicted with vomiting and diarrhea. Loose bowels are quite common in the last two weeks of pregnancy, although occasionally constipation occurs.

Gestation Period

Kittens are born approximately nine weeks, or 63 days, from the time of conception. A variation of a few days more or less, such as 61 or 65 days, is quite common. If she was with the

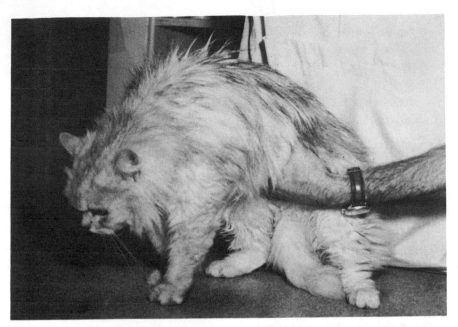

Your veterinarian can determine the condition of a cat's organs by palpation with his experienced fingers. Such an examination of a pregnant female can be useful to help in determining how many kittens are to be expected. Photo by Louise Van der Meid.

male for several days, you have about a week of "expectation," counting the variability of carrying time.

Some individual females seem to have the same carrying time for each litter. It helps if you know from her past performances that a certain cat usually has her kittens earlier or later than nine weeks. If a female is more than a day or two overdue—65 days from the last possible breeding date—it would be well to have her checked by a veterinarian. Something may have gone wrong, making his help necessary. Occasionally, a female will have one or more kittens one day and another one, or more, as long as 48 hours after the arrival of the first. This could possibly be the natural result of different conception times, if the kittens are all alive. More often, if more than 12 hours have elapsed between the arrival of the first kitten and the last, the later ones will be dead. Sometimes the dead can be delivered normally; at other times surgical help is needed. This is explained in the section on delivery.

While Persian cats *can* have any number of kittens in a litter, three or four is the average. Many have only two, and some have only one. More than five or six is not common. The females who do have large litters quite often come from a large litter themselves, or from a family tree that shows this tendency.

It has been noted that some individual females tend to have about the same size litters each time.

As in everything regarding cats, there often are more exceptions than there are those who fit any rule, so it is difficult to predict what is "normal" for any particular individual.

False pregnancy is a condition in which a female exhibits all the symptoms of pregnancy, yet no offspring result, because she has never conceived them. It is a fairly common occurrence with dogs, but extremely rare with cats.

Miscarriage

There are, however, circumstances in true pregnancy that would resemble, and possibly be diagnosed as, false pregnancy if the cat had not been checked previously to verify conception. Miscarriage can occur at any time in the nine weeks' carrying time, sometimes without your knowledge. The embryos may have been either passed out or resorbed somewhere along the line. In cases where it was known that the cat was indeed pregnant, these were the circumstances involved when no kittens arrived at the proper time.

The size of each fetus and its placenta, not counting the water sac, is only about half the size of your thumb, at four to five weeks. This is about the time that the death of the fetus is most likely to occur. If it is passed out, the solid part may be unnoticed in the sandpan or done away with by the mother.

The fetuses and other material in the womb can liquefy and then be absorbed into the mother's system. If the liquid is passed instead of being absorbed, it could be cleaned off by her without your noticing.

Causes of death of kittens in the fetal stages are varied. The embryo may be weak to begin with, or may not be developing properly, and so die. The mother may have a slight uterine infection which would kill the kittens but not affect her condition enough for you to be aware of it.

Some females just seem to have a uterus which will not keep kittens in it past a certain time. No infection is necessarily involved. A course of antibiotics while the uterus is still active after miscarriage might eliminate problems in the next litter, if infection is suspected.

The breeding to a particular sire may be one that has lethal (or Rh type) factors which would kill the fetuses. If mated to a different male, the kittens would survive.

Shock or injury can cause miscarriage or premature delivery, but this is seldom a factor in the early stages.

Close-to-term miscarriages can be caused for the same reasons as those occurring early in pregnancy. Usually the mass is expelled with labor symptoms and is sizeable enough to be noticed. Sometimes a female will carry to full term undeveloped kittens that have died some time beforehand, in various stages of development. It is possible for one or more full-term live kittens to be delivered along with those that have not developed fully.

In any miscarriage or presence of dead fetuses or kittens in the uterus, there is always the danger of having the mother cat becoming poisoned or developing a chronic uterine infection.

Repeated miscarriages indicate that a cat should be spayed. It is not likely that kittens ever will result from her, and you may have a very sick or a dead female instead, if you persist.

Premature Kittens

Some females are just too full of kittens to carry them quite full term. The only time these girls carry successfully is if they just happen to conceive fewer babies.

Kittens born prematurely by more than one or two days generally have a poor chance of survival. When born, they not only look small and naked compared to full-term kittens—they are. They do not have enough hair on or enough fat under their skins to keep body heat in or protect them from chilling in the air. These are the things that fill out in the last week of uterine containment. The premature kitten's organs are not fully ready to work on their own. They are usually too weak to nurse, and sometimes the swallowing mechanism is not yet operating. You

Shaded male owned by Mr. and Mrs. J. Wysocki: **TR. CH. DEARHEART TERRY OF DONEGAI.** Sire: **Dbl. Ch. Mr. Rhett Butler;** dam: **Reene's Marie of Dearheart. Photo by Gordon Laughner.**

may try having them nurse from the mother, but hold them in your hand or wrap them up so that they do not get chilled.

Complete details on how to care for premature kittens is in the section on Delivery. Each day of life improves their chances for survival.

Drying Up Milk

A question that is often asked is: "How do you dry up female cats?" Mother cats that suddenly have no kittens to nurse as a result of miscarriage or death or departure of the kittens are often uncomfortably full of milk.

There is no effective way to assist in the drying up process. If there is no further stimulus, such as the nursing of kittens, the milk glands gradually stop producing of their own accord.

The only soothing preparation that could be put on the breasts of a cat would be olive oil or white vaseline. These will not harm her if she washes them off (as she no doubt will). Withhold milk and milk products.

Occasionally a breast will become infected, which, of course, requires veterinary treatment.

VIII

THE BIRTH OF A KITTEN

Fact and Fancy

The most tragic error of all, which costs the lives of many kittens and their mothers, is the notion that *all* female cats can have their kittens better without human assistance.

This is a type of thinking left over from the time when even human birth processes were considered a mystery and mothers to be beyond help. It is ridiculous to apply that sort of thinking in this day and age, when we have access to experienced and sympathetic professional aid. Besides, the opportunity to be present at the very onset of life itself is an experience that never ceases to produce in me the feeling of being closer to the Creator for a moment.

It *is* possible for a female cat to deliver her kittens and get them out of their sacs in time to live, with *no* help.

It is also *very possible* that she might need your assistance, or that of a veterinarian. In any case, it is always wise to alert your veterinarian as to the approximate time the kittens are due so that he will be more readily available if you should need him.

In breeding toward the desired standard (for long-haired cats especially) we are interested in having kittens with large, broad heads and short, cobby bodies. A kitten with a big head has a hard time coming into the world from his short-bodied mother.

Long-haired cats have become used to your taking care of all their wants, and they are very attached to their owners and particularly want your companionship when something unusual, such as having kittens, is afoot.

Preliminaries

In my experience with expectant mothers, when the time for kittens is near they will not let me out of their sight. This can become rather inconvenient if it goes on, as it can, for several days before the kittens actually arrive.

Long before the time the kittens are due, the prospective mother will have been looking for a likely "nest." Her ideas on the subject can be quite different from what you have in mind as a suitable place.

They jump in any drawer or enclosure, however small, that is left open. Some cats can open doors and drawers for themselves. Care must be taken to see that the mother cat does not get shut in some place by mistake.

Many of them not only try out drawers and cupboards for size but also excavate their contents or rip them in their zeal to arrange a proper "nest."

Get a fairly large cardboard box ready, anyway. Put it in a dark, protected spot, such as under a table or in a closet or cupboard. When the time actually comes, the mother can usually be persuaded to make use of it, at least to deliver the kittens in. She may even be pleased with it beforehand.

Some females will grab up and try to drag off to the box any size kitten to make a "baby" of when their time is near. One of our girls, Susette, a very tiny cat, would suddenly remember at that time that her grown-up daughter, Marie, was once her kitten. Marie, although not very large, was considerably bigger than Susette. Nevertheless, she would be hauled away by the nape of the neck, although screaming her protests to her very determined mother.

Ahead of kittening time, clean off any waxy secretion from the prospective mother's nipples. A little oil will soften it for easy removal. Also clip short the fur on her entire stomach. If the fur is short around each nipple, it will make it easier for the newborn to find them and will prevent milk-soaked fur from caking over the nipples, which can cause a lot of trouble. Check nipple condition and access often after the babies arrive, as their rooting and kneading will sometimes cause a cap to form over the nipple and shut off the milk supply.

There generally is a period of several hours of preliminary contractions and a slight discharge of fluid before any real labor starts. If you happen not to be available, many females will hold back delivery as long as they can to wait until you *are* there.

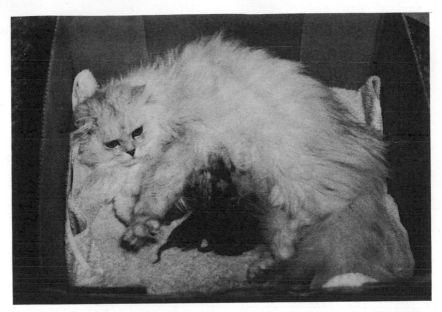

Chinchilla Persian **MISTRESS MARY** with her newborn Silver kittens. The box is large enough for the mother's comfort but small enough to be draft-free when mother leaves. Photo by Louise Van der Meid.

Delivery Tips

The delivery box should not be too deep. A box with high sides is awkward to reach down into in case she needs assistance.

Besides, she likes to be able to see who or what might be approaching by just lifting her head above the top. It should be wide and long enough for her to stretch out comfortably. The bottom of the box should be covered with several layers of newspaper sections. (I put a soft cloth on top of the newspapers for my mother cats to knead and arrange before birth time.) When she begins to labor, take everything out except the paper, until after all the babies arrive. Newspaper absorbs any fluid expelled, and the wet portions can be disposed of as you go along to keep the bed dry between the arrival of each kitten. Some females like to brace themselves against the sides of the box to get more leverage to push.

The intervals between kitten births are variable. They may be spaced anywhere from ten minutes to two or more hours apart.

The mother might enjoy a drink of water or warm milk while she is resting.

It is well to remove the already-born babies from the labor box when the mother is about to deliver another one. Have a little semi-covered, warmly lined box at hand to put them in, out of her way. You may give them back to her between kittens.

Some of my mothers will get out of the box in the midst of having their kittens if I try to leave them alone for a minute. I usually arrange to have some other person there with me to keep her company if it should become necessary to leave. We have spent many uncomfortable hours taking turns on the floor of our bedroom closet (which all our mother cats feel is the proper place to have kittens in our house). Lately we have moved the box into a more comfortable place for *us*, once labor has started, until all the kittens are born.

Purring

Cats often purr loudly before and during the kittening. This purr sounds different from that which denotes contentment. Cats purr this way at other times, too; when they are nervous, upset, or in pain, for example.

Taking Stock of the Situation

A cat's uterus has two sides, or "horns". It is shaped like a short-stemmed letter "Y." Kittens usually are carried in both sides. The kittens are packed in tightly, like peas in two pods, at the time of birth. Each kitten born has a 50-50 chance of being presented for delivery hind-end first (breech). If the head is first, the birth is easier. The shape of the head is more suited to forcing its passage through the pelvis. A tail or feet do not bring enough pressure to bear to open a passageway. There is no way to turn a kitten end-for-end inside the mother, because the area is too cramped after the uterus has contracted around the fetus during labor. The only remote possibility of doing this is for the veterinarian to slip the kitten around into the other side, or "horn," which then would put him in head-first position.

Breech Birth

You can help to get the kitten out if it is coming "breech." Grasp as much of the kitten's body as you can. Use a piece of gauze or a washcloth to prevent it from slipping. Occasionally the buttocks are presented first, with the legs folded back. In this case an attempt can be made to straighten the legs out. Then pull gently and steadily, as the mother pushes. If possible, have someone else hold the mother cat's head to keep her from biting at you due to the pain of delivery.

The Sac and the Placenta (Afterbirth)

Each kitten is completely enclosed in a sac, or membranous bag filled with liquid. The kitten "swims" around inside it. The kitten gets his oxygen (and food) supply before birth from the mother cat. The placenta ("afterbirth") is attached to the mother's uterus. The kitten in the sac is connected to the placenta by the umbilical cord, which is about two inches long and is the pipeline from the placenta. At the time of birth, the uterus begins to contract, pushing the kitten downward for his entrance into the world. The placenta detaches from its place on the uterus wall at that time, and then the kitten is on its own.

Removing the Sac

There is still enough oxygen left in the blood of the placenta to supply the kitten for a reasonable time; however, if the birth is delayed too long, the kitten will smother before birth. It is most important to break open the sac the kitten is enclosed in and clear the kitten's nose and mouth to the air. Wait a moment to see if the mother cat will do this with her tongue. If she does not do it quickly, do it yourself by tearing the membrane and wiping the kitten's face with a cloth. Detaching the kittens from the placenta by "cutting the cord" can wait in favor of getting the kittens to breathe.

Stimulating Circulation

The mother cat washes and tumbles the kittens about very vigorously as soon as they are born, for several purposes. The hard washing makes the baby complain loudly, which gets air into his lungs. It also stimulates the circulation and dries the wet fur. You can accomplish the same thing by rubbing the kitten briskly, head held down, with a corner of a Turkish towel —make him yell!

Removing Fluid from Lungs

A kitten sometimes needs to have fluid removed from his lungs by shaking him. Hold him in your hand with his back against your palm. Put his head face down between your first two fingers. Hold kitten's head *firmly* with your knuckles. Place your thumb and other fingers around his body. Then swing your hand downward. This will make him gasp, taking in air; also, gravity will help pull the fluid and mucus out of his lungs. Wipe it off as it appears. Repeat the shaking and wiping process until his breathing is quiet. Hold the kitten close to your ear and listen for rasping or rattling noises which mean the fluid is present. Check his tongue to see if he is getting enough oxygen throughout his system. A bright red means he has enough oxygen in his bloodstream; a blue tongue indicates that he is not receiving enough oxygen.

The shaking procedure and the brisk rubbing with a towel can be alternated and repeated to get a weak baby breathing normally. Get him dry. Keep him warm.

Severing the Cord

The mother cat severs the cord by eating the afterbirth and cord to the proper length. She stops chewing from 3/4 of an inch to one inch from the kitten's body.

Her teeth crush the open end of the cord so that it does not continue to bleed. If, instead, *you* do the "cutting of the cord," use a tearing motion, holding the end toward the body for a moment until the bleeding slackens. A dull scissors to crush and seal the blood vessels in the cord may be used instead. Be sure to allow plenty of distance between the cut and the body of the kitten. The cord can be trimmed to the proper length with sharp scissors after it dries. The end may be tied with a piece of thread if bleeding persists. A drop of disinfectant may be placed on the open end.

Eating the Placenta   (Afterbirth)

A mother cat's purpose in eating the placenta is to provide her with liquid and nourishment between births. The placenta has various hormone substances that her system needs, and it acts as a physic to clear out wastes.

In the wild state, a mother cat would be unable to hunt for food and water for herself for a few days after giving birth, and the eating of the placentas would provide enough nourishment to carry her through that time. In the case of a domesticated cat, however, it is not necessary for her to eat all of the placentas. Take them away after the first two are eaten. Each kitten has an individual placenta. Be sure that each one is accounted for. If they are not delivered and remain in the uterus, they can cause infection.

After all the kittens arrive, clean up the box and put in soft cloths for the bed. Use flannel or sheeting so the kittens can get some traction to move. Do not use a Turkish towel or other loosely woven material in which their claws will catch. Provide warm milk and food for the mother right in the bed, after she has settled down. Many mothers prefer to eat this way for a few days.

Malformations

Intestines outside the Body

Occasionally kittens arrive with the intestines outside the body. This is thought by some people to be caused by baby's being injured by the birth itself, or by the mother's biting the cord off too short. This is not the way it happens. The condition is due to the fact that the sides of the stomach wall do not knit together in the middle as they should before birth. It is a fault in the development of the embryo. Nothing can be done to remedy this situation unless the unclosed gap is very small and the intestines, uncontaminated, can be put back right away and confined by a stitch or two. Kittens with this condition are born alive and may remain alive for some time, contrary to expectation.

Cleft Palate

Another malformation, which cannot be remedied, is a cleft palate. This is a condition in which the roof of the mouth is not closed but opens directly into the nose. Kittens of this type cannot nurse and will not survive. It can be detected by looking into their mouths; definite evidence of cleft palate is given if the milk starts coming out of their nostrils. Cleft palate is sometimes, though not always, accompanied by a malformation of the hind legs (turned the wrong way). There is no solution to this except to destroy the kitten. As this is more likely than not to be an inherited defect, rather than one due to improper development of the cells in the embryo, it is not desirable to repeat the breeding.

Open Eyes

The eyes of a newborn kitten are not ready to be exposed to the air, and kittens born with their eyes open may be blind. Many times such a condition is due to the fact that part of the firm edge of the upper (or, occasionally, the lower) eyelid is not formed properly, resulting in failure of the eyelids to come together to protect the eye. Sometimes the eye itself is not affected, if light is kept from it, but trouble with hairs from above or below the eyelid poking into the eye will ensue as time goes on, causing discomfort. If such a condition should exist in a particularly valuable animal, it can sometimes be corrected by surgery.

It is possible that this condition can result from lack of proper vitamin intake by the expectant mother cat. It is also possible that this is an hereditary defect and, as such, should not be perpetuated. The criterion, I would say, should be whether this is an isolated occurrence in a particular line or whether others of the family have the same problem. The decision must be made, based on known facts and prior experience, as to whether the kitten should be put to sleep at once or further development in future breeding awaited.

Faulty Development of Hindquarters

Another possible malformation may be evidenced by the kitten that does not seem able to walk properly, usually because of faulty development of the muscles of the hindquarters. This, too, can be the result of either individual weakness, which will be out-grown, or inherited tendencies. Only time and experience will tell which is the cause.

Euthanasia (Painless Destruction)

Kittens born with the malformation of cleft palate or with other debilitating defects that will not respond to treatment should be given a merciful death, preferably by your veterinarian. If you cannot reach your veterinarian, the responsibility for relieving the cat of its life falls on you. You can kill a kitten quickly and painlessly by holding it, in a bag, over a jet of a gas range or the exhaust pipe of an automobile. You can also drown it in a covered jar full of water; this last procedure is the least preferable, obviously.

Rush to the Veterinarian!

When a female has been in hard labor (contractions severe enough to make her whiskers pull together) for two hours and no kittens have arrived, take her to your veterinarian. She prob-ably needs his help for delivery. If you are in any doubt, even earlier, consult him about the situation immediately.

The uterus of some females does not have the required "tone," or push power, to expel the kittens. Injections of posterior pituitary extract can be given in the case of contractions of the uterus too weak to move the kittens downward and out. This type of injection may be repeated at intervals. It should not be given until the cervix is completely dilated by preliminary labor stages. These weak contractions may go on for some time. A ruptured uterus might result if a stimulant is given too soon. If the mother cat's uterus does not respond to this stimulus sufficiently, there is no way to get the kittens out except by surgery.

Sometimes the head or kitten is too large to go through the pelvis. If help of a professional nature is not given in time, the kitten will die, and others of the litter due to follow must wait too long, so that their placentas separate from the uterus and they, too, will die in the womb for lack of oxygen.

A dead kitten is an *immediate* source of possible infection to the mother cat. If untreated, she may die of this infection or be unable ever to have any more kittens.

If a mother cat has been in labor a long time trying to deliver a dead kitten, and surgery is required, she may be too weak from pain and effort to survive the anesthetic. Further, if she has become poisoned from the presence of one or more dead kittens in the uterus, she is a poor risk for surgery.

There are two possible solutions to the situation arising when the kitten is unable to pass through the opening between the pelvic bones or when the mother's uterus does not have the "push" power to expel it:

1. *Use of Forceps*

An expert veterinarian can remove the kitten, which is probably already dead by this time, carefully extracting it little by little with forceps. As the mother must be under anesthetic for him to do this, it will be necessary to attempt to remove the remaining kittens the same way. They usually will not survive this method of delivery. This method is seldom used if there are more than two kittens present in the uterus.

2. *Caesarian Section*

A Caesarian section can be performed, and is always indicated, if any of the kittens has a chance of being alive and the mother is in good condition. Anesthesia is required for either forceps delivery or Caesarian section. However, in the Caesarian operation, there is the additional strain and shock to the mother when, of necessity, the uterus is exposed to the air.

It is up to the veterinarian to make the decision as to which is the better method, according to the individual circumstances. His primary concern is for the life and well being of the mother cat, and that should be yours, too.

Except for very unusual circumstances, there can always be another litter of kittens. Many cats have survived several Caesarian sections.

Planned Caesarian

Occasionally, as it is with human beings, there are certain

mother cats that will always require surgery for delivery of kittens. These should be planned for ahead of time. A single accurate breeding date is necessary to insure success. Prematurely born Persian kittens do not stand a good chance of survival. A few days' difference provides them with sufficient fat and fur to keep heat loss in the newborn at a minimum.

The circumstances that require repeated surgery are as follows:

If the pelvic bone and muscle structure are too rigid to permit sufficient separation to allow passage of a kitten. Some females have a male-type pelvic construction. This can also become the condition if a female is too old before having her first litter. An experienced veterinarian can diagnose this continuing complication when the first Caesarian is done.

Time is of the essence, of course, in any question of birth—life and death are separated by seconds. So, if you know from past experience that the foregoing problems may arise, prompt action will result in live kittens—and an alive mother cat.

The mother cat who has had an anesthetic for delivery is not herself until half a day to a day after the delivery. Provisions have to be made for the feeding and care of the babies. If you put the babies with her before she has completely recovered from the anesthetic, they might hurt her and she might bite them, not realizing fully what is going on.

A side, or flank, incision for Caesarians is the most satisfactory. The mother can lie comfortably on one side and not have a sore spot near any nipple.

Motherless Newborn

If your best efforts and those of your veterinarian fail and you have orphan kittens, try to find another mother cat who will take the babies. No one should refuse a call for help in this situation. A baby kitten needs a mother cat for survival, if at all possible. Most mother cats will accept orphans if you rub the smell of her own on the newcomers. Always offer her the kitten bottom first—no mother cat can ignore a bottom to clean! Also helpful is placing the kitten for her to "find." Her maternal instinct, aroused by the helpless one's crying, will usually prompt her to take it to her bosom without question.

It is well to attempt to breed two females so that their kittens will arrive at approximately the same time. I try to do this routinely, particularly if a Caesarian is likely to be in the offing.

Care of the Orphaned, Weak, or Premature Kitten

The main need of newborn kittens is to be dried thoroughly and kept warm. You can put them in an old wool sock, sweater sleeve, glove, or mitten. Drop them down inside. The wool is porous enough so they will get air. A piece of fur is also good to wrap kittens in. They can then be kept in a small deep box, basket, or drawer. A purse sometimes fills the bill.

A heating pad on very low heat, or a hot water bottle (an ordinary bottle kept filled with warm water makes a good substitute) can be put in with the babies to keep them warm, or they can be kept in a heavy-bottomed box placed over the pilot light of a gas range. Be careful not to get them too hot.

Very little milk is required at first. A few drops of a mixture of half canned milk and half warm water is enough at a time. This mixture should be given every hour or two around the clock until the mother takes over.

However, do not try to feed a newborn kitten that is too weak to swallow, or you will drown it in milk. A kitten will continue to gain strength without feeding for a period of several hours, if it is kept warm. This strength comes from the glycogen which was stored in his liver before birth. Many babies have been lost due to over-anxious feeding before their swallowing mechanism was strong enough to work.

A tiny kitten is unable to pass urine or move his bowels without assistance. Gently massage the area with a piece of damp cotton each time you feed him. Keep stroking until elimination stops.

If you do not feel that you would be willing to try to cope with possible problems, do not breed your female. I do not wish to imply that your cat will always have difficulties; however, any cat can have a birth problem at any time. To me, the difficulties, if overcome, should make one proud to have been able to help little creatures which could not help themselves. If it so happens that your efforts are in vain—you tried your best! More than that no one can do, and there should be no self-reproach.

IX

BRINGING UP THE CHILDREN

The Bed

A deeper box is better for a permanent kitten bed. I cut a wide opening in one side so that the mother can not only walk in but also see out. Cut it to about four inches above the bedding so that the kittens can't crawl or fall out. As they get older, they can get out of anything that is uncovered. If they can stretch their paws to reach to the top of it, they will pull themselves up and over.

Quite a few mother cats decide, somewhere along the line after their kittens are born, to move the babies. There can be many reasons for this desire. The box location may be too light or too dark or too hot or too cold for the kittens' welfare at the time, in her estimation. She may feel the kittens are in some danger from too much viewing or handling. A common reason is that the box is too small for her to stretch out comfortably to nurse her babies.

Then, too, she may feel too hot with the babies in close quarters or on heavy bedding. A mother sometimes moves her kittens to the litter box for its coolness. This is most undesirable, as the kittens get the litter in their faces and could smother. I have had some mothers insist on putting them back there, again and again. I finally solved the problem by removing most of the litter and covering the rest with a thin piece of old sheet tucked in. This satisfies the mother and protects the kittens.

If the box is too large, it may be drafty and the kittens will get cold when the mother leaves them.

First-time mothers sometimes are bewildered by their new responsibilities, and do not stay with the kittens as they should, unless you are there. This phase usually passes in a day or so. Encourage the new mother to stay in the box. If she won't remain with them, see that the kittens are kept warm.

Enough Milk

Sometimes a mother seems to sense that she hasn't enough milk or hasn't any milk at all, and will not stay with the babies. Or she may be feverish for some reason. Check that possibility first, and try to determine the cause. If she does have a fever, she may need a veterinarian's attention.

Cats are naturally very good mothers, so if one neglects or moves her kittens, there is usually a good reason for it. Try to find out what is disturbing her.

Born Blind

Kittens are born blind. The eyes open at one week to ten days of age. Kittens should be kept in a dark place until their eyesight is fully developed, gradually increasing the amount of exposure to light. If the eyelids stick back together, or matter collects after opening, bathe the eyes with cotton soaked in a mild boric acid solution (1 teaspoon to 8 ounces of water) or just warm water. If the condition persists, bathe the eyes and apply a cat eye ointment or drops.

Supplemental Nursing

Check the kittens often during the first few days to see that they are getting enough food. They should feel fully packed and rounded within 24 hours after birth. If it should be necessary to supplement by hand-feeding, a temporary formula of half evaporated milk and half water may be given from an eye dropper or bottle. Strangely enough, not all brands of canned milk are well tolerated. If you are using one that agrees with your kitten, stay with it. If the kitten shows signs of gastric distress, try a different kind of milk or add a small amount (one teaspoon to eight ounces) of limewater. A small amount of white Karo Syrup and vitamins should be added if the necessity to hand-feed continues for any length of time. Frequency of feeding depends upon age and intake, on the basis of two- to four-hour intervals. For further details, refer to the section on Motherless Newborn.

Only a general guide can be given to the growth progress of

The mid-section of a newborn kitten should look like this within 24 hours if it is getting enough to eat. Photo by Louise Van der Meid.

a baby kitten. Most Persian kittens should double their birth weight at one week of age, and gain four ounces each week for the next two weeks.

When a kitten is three weeks old, the nursing (or bottle feeding) can be supplemented with food. Canned strained baby meat, egg yolk, or cottage cheese can be fed now. Also, soft scrapings from lean beef make a good starter diet. A kitten has plenty of sharp little teeth to chew with, though, so change to a coarser style of meat before long.

At four to five weeks of age, a kitten should eat about a teaspoonful of solid food per day. His capacity should gradually increase to a tablespoonful at eight weeks. The food and milk should be given in small amounts, four of five times daily.

It is not necessary for you to supplement with food at three weeks, if the babies are doing well. They will gradually start

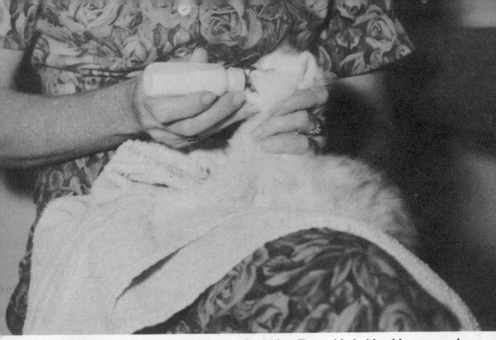

Do not lay a kitten on his back to feed him. To avoid choking him, approximate his natural nursing position. The author here feeds a four-week-old baby from a bottle. Photo by Louise Van der Meid.

getting into their mother's food when they are able to climb out of the box at about four weeks.

Toilet Needs and Weaning

The mother cares for all the kittens' toilet needs until they are big enough to climb into the litter box. From this time on, they gradually start to eat, lap milk, and go to the box at mother's direction, with little assistance from you. Weaning usually is complete by the time the kitten is six to eight weeks of age.

A kitten should be eating entirely independently of his mother for at least a week before he goes to a new home.

Feline Enteritis Vaccination

A kitten will hold an immunity to feline enteritis (the immunization is obtained from his mother's milk, if she has been immunized) up to two weeks after he is weaned. After that, he can contract it if he is not vaccinated. It is important that this be done as soon as possible. If he has been eating well for a week beforehand, eight weeks is the recommended age for vaccination.

The usual method is a series of two shots, given a week to ten days apart. The kitten starts to build up immunity right away, and the peak is reached shortly after the second shot is given. There is a one-shot vaccination, which is comparatively new in usage; however, the two-shot method has been found by long experience to be one of the most effective of all animal vaccinations, so it is preferred.

Mother Is Teacher

The mother cat teaches the kittens many things by example. Kittens get very adventuresome at about five weeks, and often will not mind when mother calls. The mother chirps and scolds the babies to keep them in line. Usually, by the time the kittens are eight weeks old, she has become reconciled to the fact that they are getting grown-up enough to be on their own without her constant supervision.

Time to Be Practical

As mentioned earlier, the mother, contrary to popular belief, can come in season again anytime shortly after having kittens, so accidental breeding must be guarded against. Only one litter a year is advised, except in unusual cases where the female can become more rundown by constant "calling" than by having another family. The drain on the mother cat's system is heaviest when she is nursing, and she should be watched for signs of calcium deficiency, or eclampsia, particularly around the time the kittens are three to four weeks old, or if the litter is large. See the suggestions for vitamin and calcium supplements in the section on Feeding.

One cat is fun—the more cats, the more fun—within limits, of course. If you have too many, you can't give each one the individual attention and drawing-out it deserves.

How many cats are "too many" is entirely dependent upon the circumstances and situation of the individual owner. I always advise anyone to proceed slowly until he has an idea of what problems might be involved in having a group of cats. You should clearly understand, also, the demands on your time and purse before you decide that you must keep all of the kittens from your cat's first litter. Darling and special they are, indeed, but if you keep all of them, you probably will not have room to take on any more next year.

You should have little trouble selling Persian kittens. Your petshop owner may be interested in buying one. Word of mouth is usually the best advertisement, and friends who know that your Persian has had kittens will tell others. A notice placed on the bulletin board of your neighborhood market or veterinarian's office may also be used to good advantage in selling kittens. An ad in your local newspaper or a magazine for pet sales should bring results.

If you have male and female unaltered cats, whatever their relationship to each other, they will probably mate with or without your approval. A cat of either sex is capable of reproducing as soon as permanent teeth have been cut. This can be as early as five months.

If you do want to have and enjoy two or more kittens or cats stick to the same sex, or have them altered so you will be able to control the number of new additions to the household.

Will Your Male Hurt the Kittens?

If your male Persian cat has been a house pet and is acquainted with the female who is to have kittens, there is little, if any, chance of his even thinking of harming the babies. More than likely, he will be afraid of them.

I have never known any of my toms to show the least hostility towards kittens. They usually will avoid any contact with them until they are of toddling age.

Occasionally, a young male will get carried away playing chase with a run-about-size kitten. The baby yells if the male gets too rough, and he quits immediately. The mother cat will come to deal with the situation anytime a kitten hollers "help."

X

SUSTAINING THE INNER CAT

Feeding

If possible, feed any newly-acquired cat or kitten what he has been used to eating. Change diet and water gradually to avoid digestive upset and diarrhea. If there is a difference in your water supply, use distilled water at first, then mix your tap water with it little by little. Quite often a cat in new surroundings is not too interested in food. Exploration and shakedown comes first! Do not be alarmed if this is the case. Try later with fresh food— a healthy animal soon will be hungry.

A young kitten should be fed four times a day. If you prefer, leave a little food down all the time, keeping it fresh, of course. Babies eat a little, play and sleep, and then eat a little more. Kittens from four to eight months old can be fed on a more regular three-meals-a-day basis. The amount per day is from two to three tablespoonfuls. A kitten's growth pattern is variable, so adjust the amount of food to his appetite and size. The adult cat needs only morning and evening feedings, or just an evening meal. However, many individuals prefer to eat three smaller meals per day. Suit both your desires and his. Naturally, a pregnant female or nursing mother requires more food, extra calcium, and vitamins. An adult female will eat about eight to ten ounces of food a day. Males will eat a little more.

The amount of food taken at any one time and the frequency of meals are governed by individual requirements and tastes. A cat will not overeat, except occasionally of special delicacies such as chicken, turkey, shrimp, or fresh raw liver.

The Fussy Eater

Pet cats have a reputation for being fussy eaters. They will relish a certain type or brand of food one day and refuse it the next. On the other hand, in some cats there is a strong tendency to want only fish, liver, kidney, or whatever happens to be his particular fancy. Fortunately, in the last few years so many different kinds of foods have become available that any cat should be able to be satisfied, tastewise, and well-nourished if he doesn't eat one thing only. Sometimes you can outwit a finicky cat by mixing the kind of food he wants to eat with the kind of food you want him to eat.

The Balanced Diet

I feel that a varied, well-balanced diet is very important for health and beauty. A proper diet requires a high proportion, at least 20%, of protein, and 25% fats and fatty acids. In addition to the other vitamins, cats need more Vitamin B_1, B_{12}, and other B-complex vitamins than any other animal. To see that your cat is provided these and all the other necessary elements, try to imagine in general what a cat would eat if unconfined. In the wild state, fish, birds, and other vegetable-grain eaters, such as rabbits and mice, are eaten nearly entirely. It follows, then, that meat with fat, organs, cereal, bonemeal, certain vegetables (to a very minor degree), dairy products, fish, and eggs, can all have a place in your cat's diet. Some cats have loose bowels from drinking milk. If so, other dairy products, such as cheese and butter, can be substituted. It is not necessary for cats to have milk itself. Access to green growth, such as coarse-bladed grass, also is desirable. It is used by cats in nature as an emetic to cause vomiting to get rid of something not wanted in their digestive systems, such as hair balls.

How Cats Like to Be Served — and Why

Whether or not he will eat the solid food you offer your cat depends a great deal on its being of an attractive size and shape to him. Cats like to reach out with their teeth and grab what they are going to chew. Pile the pieces in a mound so he can nab each one off easily. Cut the meat to a size that will fit into his mouth for chewing without choking him.

Some cats take their food from the dish and put it on the floor before eating it. They prefer to deal with each one in turn; this method completely separates the pieces they are going to eat from all the other pieces. Most cats do not like to get their muzzles and noses into the food to eat it. If the food is smaller in size to begin with, such as ground meat, form it into little balls of the right size before serving.

Food should be served on a shallow or flat plate or saucer. There should be a clean one for each meal. Either mound food up or put it around the edge of the dish for easy access. Cats do not relish any type of food that sticks to the roof of the mouth while being chewed. Cat meal in the kibble size seems to be quite attractive, even if served dry. It is nutritious, good for jaw development, and helps prevent tartar from forming on the teeth.

Foods and Flavors Cats Enjoy

Tomato juice and other tomato products are good sources of Vitamin C. Tomato flavor is very well liked by many cats. Most cats like a little saltiness to their food. A little iodized salt in or on the food can help prevent iodine deficiency. It has been suspected that this lack might affect the conception and carrying to term of kittens, so it is a good precaution.

Many cats like the flavor of garlic, although the theory that feeding your cat garlic will keep it free of worms is another old wives' tale. (Treatment for worms is described in the section on Health.)

Cats seem to prefer food with an odor that is strong to us; kidney and fish are examples. Some cats do not care for fish at all; others love it in any form. Almost all cats like kidney, either canned or raw. It is a good standby if a cat will not eat anything else. Kidney, however, is not a sufficiently complete food for a cat to eat, exclusive of all other food, over a long period of time. Some of the other organ meats, such as melts, are sources of many valuable vitamins and minerals, but do not have sufficient protein value, either. However, heart meat, also popular with cats, is muscle meat. It and all other types of beef, veal, lamb, or mutton muscle meat are sources of high-quality protein, whether raw or cooked. Pork muscle meat must be well cooked for animals as well as humans.

Liver is well liked. A little raw liver given regularly is an essential item in the feeding of cats. There is a necessary vitamin faction in raw liver that cannot be obtained in any other manner. But too much raw liver at a time is likely to produce loose bowels, so feed it cautiously to see what the effect might be.

Chicken is good for cats. Chicken bones are not. The bones are porous and may splinter while being chewed. A cat can get a tooth caught in this type of bone and be very uncomfortable, even choke, until the bone is detached.

All types of fish and sea food may be fed, but only as a portion of the diet. Be careful of the splintery bones that are present in fish. Red meat tuna is very well liked. There have been cases where a severe Vitamin E deficiency disease, called "yellow fat disease," or steatitis, has caused the death of cats whose diet was largely or entirely red meat tuna. Most of the manufacturers have now added Vitamin E to their product, but it is still advisable not to let it be a cat's main food.

Vitamin Supplements

Vitamin supplements should be given in order to eliminate any possibility of deficiency in the diet. They also give added support to kitten and young adult growth stages, pregnant females, and nursing mothers. There are liquid products with droppers (plastic preferred, in case they are accidentally bitten) or powdered forms to sprinkle on food. Nursing baby kittens, if they are at all weak, can be given a few drops of an all-vitamin supplement daily.

To prevent eclampsia, or excessive calcium depletion from the system of a nursing or carrying female cat (more common than supposed), a calcium Vitamin D supplement is advised. Calcium is not assimilated unless Vitamin D is also present.

Vitamin B_{12} is particularly valuable to promote the formation of red blood cells. It also makes a cat feel better and have a better appetite.

Drinking Water

Fresh water should be available to your cats and kittens at all times. They often will drink water out of flower vases, as that kind of water seems extra tasty. Aside from drinking it, many cats enjoy playing with water.

XI

CAT COMFORTS AT HOME AND ABROAD

Plumbing Fixtures

Inside sanitary conveniences must be provided for a kitten. This should consist of a fairly deep pan half-filled with sand, dirt, shredded paper, or commercial litter. I have found the litter to be the most satisfactory by far, and the deodorizing and super-absorbent qualities well justify the cost. The ashes in a fireplace are attractive to some cats for use as a toilet. See that such a habit never gets started by "cat proofing" the opening with a tight fireplace screen. You may buy a special "litter pan" in the pet shop. Adjust the amount of litter you put in the pan to your own preference and the needs of your cat. The used material in the pan can be disposed of as often as necessary, and there will be no unpleasant odor about the house. A few folds of newspaper in the bottom of the pan will increase absorption and make disposal easier.

Put the pan in a deep-sided cardboard carton or on an island of newspapers. Cats often make a great project of "covering up" and in their zeal will fling material out of the pan for some distance. If the box is too high for a small kitten to jump into, cut an entry in one side. If you have a very large home, it would be well to have a second bathroom set up for a baby. A very young kitten might not be able to reach the spot in time, as he will put off the necessary trip until the very last minute. If he has another, nearer, place to go to, it will help him avoid making "mistakes."

Put him in the pan as soon as you get him home. Let him explore from there, using it as home base. Then if you place him in the litter box after each meal, he will be house-trained to your home very quickly. Kittens are nearly always good about using the pan, and fail only when ill, frightened, or confused as to its location. If your kitten is trained to one material but you wish to change to a different type, do it gradually. Put a little of the new material with the old, gradually increasing the amount each day until the old type is entirely eliminated. When I had a disposal problem in an apartment, I trained one cat successfully from sand to toilet paper, little by little. Many apartment-dwelling cats will train themselves, or can be trained, to use the bathtub drain. This method has obvious advantages — and disadvantages.

Scratching Posts

If you provide a place that he can dig his claws into, your cat will be more likely to leave the furniture and rugs alone. A scratching post may be purchased or you can make one. It

Shaded Silver female owned by Mrs. Harold Webb: TR. CH. MESA MISS PIXYANNE. Sire: Ch. Sir Pixie of Silver Mesa; dam: Cecilia Scotia of Silver Mesa.

The tips of the cat's nails should be kept blunt with the special nail clippers available at pet stores. Photo by Louise Van der Meid.

should have a wide, heavy base to avoid tipping over. Cats like to reach out or up, and dig in. This is very good and necessary exercise and apparently greatly enjoyed by cats of all ages. The post itself should be covered with carpeting or made of a material that he can get his claws well into and then pull them out again with a satisfactory-sounding "rip." (An old wicker clothes hamper is the favorite post at our house.) A catnip smell can be used as an added attraction for the post.

Nail Clippers

The claws of a cat are retractile, so constructed that they can be extended or pulled back in their individual sheaths at will. Keep the claws of your young kitten clipped short. This will force him to jump instead of climbing "hand over hand" to get where he wants to go.

Tiny babies can hurt one another's eyes in play as they do not know yet how to keep their claws in. It is well to keep their claws blunted. Grown cats in the house can have their claws kept clipped to good advantage. This job can be done fairly easily at home with a nail clipper made especially for cat claws. Push the claw out of the sheath by pressing on the toe pad from the underside of the paw and keep it held out by holding your thumb on top. Then cut off the hooked portion as often as necessary. Do not trim too close to the quick, the pinkish area near the base of claw. The long, slender, hooked needle of bloodless growth is the cutting area. If you prefer, your veterinarian will do it for you. Some cats' claws grow very fast; others need clipping less often. Don't forget the "dewclaw," or thumb, on the front feet.

Props for Play

Toys are enjoyed by cats young and old, especially those that make a little noise. Ping-pong and other light-weight balls are great sport for a cat to play hockey with. A smooth cord or a belt with an interesting wadded paper tied to the end is better than the well-known string. Claws do not catch in the material when you "snake" it along or tie it to hang free from a door knob or chair back. Be careful not to leave threaded needles, rubber bands, or pieces of cellophane around for cats to play with, as they can be swallowed with unfortunate consequences.

Not all cats like catnip. Those that do often find the catnip box for themselves and go on a binge. Do not let them have so much that they forget themselves and get too rough.

Many cats are attracted to scents of household disinfectants, perfume, powder, and hand lotion. Cosmetic preparations with the odor of wild thyme are especially interesting to them. They will wash and roll and sometimes drool over this scent.

Cardboard houses with many doors and windows are a source of amusement for them—and you. Something of that nature may be made from a large grocery carton, or playhouses that are quite elegant may be purchased ready-made. Boxes and paper bags to get into are irresistible to most cats.

Many cats enjoy using doll furniture that is scaled to their size, such as doll cradles, playpens, and highchairs.

Carriers

A kitten or cat should be safely confined in a carrier whenever taken out of the house or away from home or yard for

Brown Tabby male owned by Mrs. C. A. Coughlin: **GR. CH. MINQUA'S GINGERSNAP OF CO-MC. Sire: Ch. Sunny-Land Calumet of Minqua; dam: Ch. Sunny-Lad Nerissa of Longhill. Bred by Mr. and Mrs. Thomas Martinke.**

any purpose. If a carrier is not available, he should be on a leash, at least. There are several reasons why a carrier is desirable and important. Not being familiar with the outside world, sudden noises or movements can startle and frighten a house cat. This can result in injury or escape, or both. Also, there is a possibility of your getting scratched or bitten during his fright.

Riding in the car is easier for both of you. The carrier can be set up high enough for him to see out, if he wants to, or covered up if he doesn't. He does not get bounced around and you do not have to watch out for him underfoot, or when car windows and doors are opened. If you have to leave him alone in the car, the carrier can be completely or partially covered so that "cat-nappers" will not be tempted. Be sure you do not leave the carrier in direct sunlight. Windows of the car should be left open slightly to provide ventilation if the cat is left alone in the car.

Also, on a trip to the veterinarian your cat is not exposed to other cats' diseases or curious strange dogs when he is in a carrier. The carrier, if left open around the house, becomes familiar to him and it then seems a place of refuge when he is exposed to unsettling experiences.

The cat carrier for Persians should be a well-ventilated type with room inside for toilet conveniences. A cloth or plastic cover can be used over the open wire top to protect him from the sun or weather, if necessary. The type pictured is very satisfactory for all traveling purposes, and also doubles as a drying cage when turned on its side. Those with a door at each end are more convenient for removing a cat that is reluctant to leave his refuge.

Shipping a Cat

Many Persian cats are shipped by air or rail, for various reasons. The type of shipping container used for this purpose must have certain features to meet the requirements of the cat's comfort and the rules of the transport company. There should be several ventilating openings in different areas to prevent suffocation. Do not put anything inside the container that the cat can dig up and so cover these openings.

The carrier or container itself should be of strong construction so that it will not be crushed or the cat escape from it en route. It should not be entirely open, leaving the cat subject to drafts on breezy airfields or train platforms.

It must be large enough to provide space for a cat's toilet and lying-down room, yet high enough for him to sit or stand upright. Send along specific instructions and provisions for care and feeding on the way, if necessary. Check with your shipping agent for complete information about other details.

Harness and Leash

A Persian cat can be trained to harness and leash. A collar is not recommended, as it can rub the fur of his ruff and cause matting and bare spots beneath, and he can pull his head out of any type collar. In one good harness, the "figure eight" type, one loop goes around the neck and the other goes under the chest, crossing over the shoulders. This is easily put on if you fasten it on top so you don't get hair caught in the buckle. If made of soft leather, there is little friction on the fur.

Safety and comfort for your cat are assured by the use of a carrier whenever you take him on a trip. The carrier should be roomy and well ventilated. Photo by Louise Van der Meid.

A young cat will consider a leash just something to play with. At first he may act as if he can't walk or even stand up in the harness. This phase passes with practice. The harness and leash can be attached outside if the yard is protected from visiting cats, dogs, and children who would find your cat helpless to defend himself or get away from harm. Be careful to tie the leash where he cannot wind it around anything and choke himself.

Call by Name and Train to a Whistle

Kittens and cats are easily toilet-trained. However, training them to do, or not to do, other things is more difficult. A very good way of training a cat to come to you whenever wanted is to always whistle for him to come to eat. Rather shrill notes seem to get the best action and are readily heard, even outdoors. A cat will also learn his name if always called by it, which is an additional protection against theft.

Outside Housing — Catteries

There may be times when you do not wish your cat to have the run of the house. Also, you may wish to separate or isolate certain ones for various reasons. It is convenient to have outside accommodations for this purpose. There is no physical hardship on a cat if proper quarters are provided.

Cattery cats usually are kept in outside houses or cages as well as in the house. Mine live in or out, according to current circumstances, with no ill effects.

Many types of construction are satisfactory, as long as the basic requirements of comfort and protection are met.

The house should be well floored and roofed (possibly insulated). Any or all of the sides and door opening may be constructed so that they can be opened or left uncovered if the weather permits. At least one or more sides should be solid or closed at all times to protect the cat from the prevailing winds.

Some apertures must be left open for ventilating purposes under all weather conditions, as moisture will collect from the cat's breathing and make the house damp if it is entirely air-tight.

Any openings, open sides, or doors should be fly-screened. This screen should be reinforced by wire mesh, a needed precaution, as screen alone can be ripped by a cat's (or dog's) claws. The wire mesh will keep your cat from getting out, and other animals cannot get in and harm him. For easier cleaning, attach the screen to the inside and have the wire on the outside. This method permits the use of chicken wire mesh which would otherwise catch the cat's fur.

Our house cats go to their outside airing via a tunnel-like passage at floor level, through our bedroom wall. This opening has a swinging flap door that is hinged for them to push either way. The door is edged with strips of rubber and has a clear plastic window in the center, as the cats were reluctant to use it until the window was added. They now can check on what or who might be awaiting them on the other side. The opening can be locked closed to keep them all in or out as circumstances require.

XII

NECESSARY CARE FOR LONGHAIRS

Grooming

Even at an early age, when combing is not strictly needed, it is well to have a daily stint with the brush and comb. This gets both you and the kitten into the habit. Careful combing will remove dead hair and open the coat. The teeth of the comb should have rounded ends which cannot tear the skin or cut the hair. All edges should be cylindrical and smooth. The comb should be made of steel and have long, slim teeth to get all the way through the fur to the skin. A comb with wide-set teeth is used first, to straighten out the tangles. Break up any large accumulations of knotted fur with one tooth, working from the bottom of the knot up. Then a somewhat finer-toothed comb is recommended to pick up loose fur and get out the small knots, which otherwise can build up to matted spots. A very fine-toothed comb is used for removing fleas or dirt, and on the shorter fur of the face. Combs are available with two sizes of teeth. Be gentle. Rough treatment will remove as much good hair as bad, and in a short time the coat will appear ragged.

Shake talcum powder into the coat. It will combine with the natural oil in the hair, and with further brushing act as a dry cleaner. An oily coat picks up dirt and dust more readily.

The kind of powder to use is baby talc or a mild unperfumed type. Corn starch, carbonate of magnesia, Fuller's Earth, or French chalk may be used instead of powder. The idea is to separate and aerate the hair, thus making it fluffy.

Pay particular attention to flanks, backs of hind legs or "pants," insides of both front and hind legs, stomach, under the chin and chest, and behind the ears. These are the potential trouble spots, especially when the undercoat is shedding out. Some people, unknowingly, just comb the top fur of the cat's back, head, and tail and find to their sorrow that the underside has become felted into a solid mattress of dead fur. Such a neglected state requires the scissors at home, or a trip to the veterinarian to be clipped or combed out, usually under anesthetic.

After the combing, brush the fur to stimulate growth and to improve gloss. When you brush, always brush the hair in the opposite direction to which it lies in order to get down to the roots. Fur around the neck, or "ruff," should be combed and brushed up and out to form an Elizabethan collar, or frame, for the face. Use a natural-bristle brush, as it causes less static electricity and does not break the hair. Never use a brush made of nylon on a long-haired cat. Do not brush or comb so vigorously that you take out the new coat along with the old one. If ears are oily, they should be cleaned gently with a cotton swab as often as necessary.

Regular grooming of a long-haired cat is very important—for your benefit and for his. There are fewer hairs around the house, especially when he is shedding. He gets accustomed to this routine to maintain his health and beauty. When he washes, there will be fewer loose hairs to be swallowed to form hairballs inside him, and less chance of sore skin due to knots and matting.

Spot Cleaning

If a Persian's coat is kept combed and brushed day by day, there will be little need for bathing. I have found the powder shampoos and cleaners to be very helpful for spot cleaning. Corn starch, corn meal, or talcum powder, also, may be used. In places where it is difficult for a cat to wash himself, the fur is likely to get a little oily—such as in front of and behind the ears, under the chin, and on down the bib, or ruff.

Part the fur and shake in cleaning material. Brush down to, and out from, the skin until soil is absorbed. Repeat application of cleaning material, if necessary, until each hair stands separately. As you work put your hand loosely over his face to shield eyes and nose from dusty irritation. The evaporating-type liquid cleaning solutions also are good. These are best applied with a soft brush or cotton.

If he gets too dirty or has fleas, an all-over bath should be given for best results. There is a great variation in coat texture

Some cats like to be held. Philip Ramsdale, Jr., holds REENE'S
PIERRE. Photo by Louise Van der Meid.

and soilability. Some cats are neat and always look spotless,
whereas others attract dirt the way some children do!

The Bath

To give a soap and water bath with the least difficulty, try
to enlist the aid of another person. An extra hand or two at the
right moment can be very helpful. First, assemble all the things
you will use for the bath, including two or three large towels.
Also, prepare your drying arrangements beforehand.

Comb the cat thoroughly and clean inside his ears with wet,
and then dry, cotton swabs. Put some kind of eye ointment or
a drop of mineral oil in his eyes to lessen possible soap irritation.

Fill the sink or tub half full of warm water before you place
him in it. Another method is to use a spray, leaving only enough
water standing to soak his feet. Getting him wet is the first
problem, as the long fur sheds water and is so thick that it takes
time to get him wet to the skin. A spoonful of mild liquid
detergent in the water makes it "wetter" and enables it to soak
into the coat more readily.

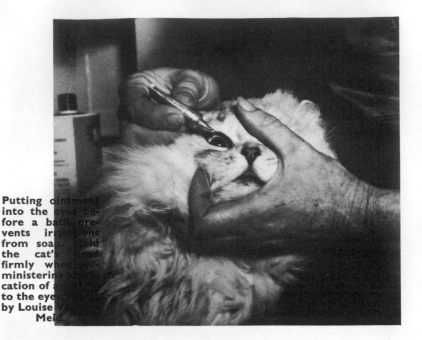

Putting ointment into the eye before a bath prevents irritations from soap. Hold the cat's head firmly when administering application of any kind to the eye. *Photo by Louise Van der Meid.*

When he is wet, gradually start working the shampoo into the skin. Do the head first, as fleas—if there are any—will congregate there and can be seen easily and removed from the short face-fur. A wash cloth is a help in cleaning around the head and face. The skin in front of the ear openings should be well scrubbed, as this is a particularly greasy spot. An old toothbrush, used gently, is good for this purpose.

Next, check the skin on top of the tail, as this too is a place which may need special attention. Often there is a brownish, oily substance, known as "stud oil" or "grease tail," exuded around the base and top ridge of the tail. This is less common on females than males, but can be present on either. If this is not removed, it discolors and separates the fur of the tail. It can form a crust on the skin, causing sores and sparse fur in this area. If this is a continuing problem, the tail (and *only* the tail) can be scrubbed with a toothbrush and detergent-type shampoo as often as necessary to prevent oil accumulation. Damp boric acid packs also are good to remove tail grease.

Pour water from a cup to get the head and face wet. Photo by Louise Van der Meid.

Work the lather through the fur to the skin. Photo by Louise Van der Meid.

Be sure to get all soap out by thorough rinsing. A spray attachment helps. Photo by Louise Van der Meid.

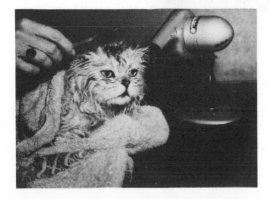

Lift fur with comb or brush to hasten drying. Photo by Louise Van der Meid.

After you have pre-washed the tail, shampoo him all over and work the lather down onto the skin. Rinse thoroughly with a spray as long as necessary to remove *all* traces of soap. Finish with a very dilute solution of white vinegar or a cream-type rinse, followed by another clear-water rinse to make sure all soap is out.

Wring out the fur by squeezing it to his body, particularly the legs, feet, and tail. Wrap him in one warm towel and dry off his face with another. This helps his morale, which may be low at this point—especially if this is his first experience. Rough-dry the rest of him with a dry towel as long as he will permit.

Drying

If the weather is warm and sunny, he can be held in your lap, put in a suitable carrier or in a cage, and kept protected from drafts or wind. As he dries, be careful that he does not get too hot from the sun on his topside. The underside and back legs take longest to get dry, unless he stands up and moves around. The natural tendency of a wet cat, however, seems to be to huddle down as small and flat as possible. Indoors, the blower end of a vacuum cleaner, a hair-dryer, the oven and a fan, or any other combination of heat and air may be used to dry him quickly.

Special Bathing Notes

If your cat should happen to get into paint, grease, tar, or oil, soak the affected parts with olive or any salad oil. Squeeze out the dirty oil with an old towel or rag, and repeat soakings until clear. Follow this with the soap-and-water treatment. Do *not* use paint thinner or cleaning fluid; it will not only burn his skin but also poison him if licked.

There is no danger in giving a soap and water bath to a healthy cat, but *a sick cat should not be bathed*. Dry-clean him, if necessary. The danger lies in not getting him completely bone-dry *to the skin* and the subsequent possibility of his becoming chilled and catching cold due to lowered resistance. Hold the fur to your face for a few moments to detect the least trace of dampness.

There are many good shampoos and cleaners on the market. If you do use any kind of medicated shampoo for fleas or skin irritations, *be sure it is a product for cats*. Read the contents on the label. Many chemicals, as listed in the section on health, are poisonous to cats. Do not take any chances. Consult your breeder or veterinarian or pet store owner for his brand recommendations.

The directions for use of medicated shampoos usually recommend leaving it on the cat's hair and skin for a certain length of time before rinsing. For the initial treatment, a wise precaution is to leave it on only a very short time—no more than a few minutes. Find out first whether your cat's skin will be irritated before you try leaving it on the full time. Cut down time considerably for kittens.

Be very careful to see that any wet cat does not become chilled or have a draft on him. Wrap him in a towel while he is still soaking wet.

If the cat is to be in a show he must be absolutely clean all over. If he requires a bath to achieve this state, you should experiment beforehand to learn how many days after bathing your cat his coat looks its best. Govern your pre-show bath date accordingly. Bathing a cat too frequently dries out his skin and dulls the luster of his fur.

It is rather an ordeal for a long-haired cat to be wet and then dried again, so he is entitled to lots of praise on his beauty and good behavior, something tasty to eat, and a nice long nap after it is all over.

Fleas

Fleas are a common problem and are very detrimental to a Persian's health and beauty. Scratching the itching flea bites ruins the coat and causes matting. Through the fleas, which are intermediate hosts to the tapeworm in cats, the animal can become infested with tapeworm. Getting rid of tapeworm after you have eradicated the fleas is a job for the veterinarian. (See section on health: Parasites.)

So-called dog fleas are larger and of a lighter brown color than cat fleas, which are dark brown or black. Then there are sand fleas. All kinds of fleas bite and live off the blood of any animal or human. Fleas bite some people readily; others they do not bother as much. If you have fleas in your house or yard, they will usually prefer to bite the dogs or cats. If your animals are away from the house for a few days, the fleas will be hungry and bite you, instead. Many persons returning from a vacation before their pets are brought home notice for the first time that there are fleas in the house.

With persistent effort, fleas can be eliminated completely from a house cat if he is always kept inside and is not exposed to re-infestation. However, if you also have a dog or a cat that does go out, it can bring in fleas to your house cat. Fleas can also be brought into the house on the clothing of persons returning to the house from outside.

To help get rid of fleas, wash all washable articles and vacuum floors and furniture frequently, particularly in the dark corners and crevices. Flea powder may be sprinkled on and left under rugs and furniture cushions. Be sure you use a flea powder that is a product made especially for *cats*. Preparations that are for dogs may kill cats. Recent developments in flea-killing preparations that are non-toxic to cats contain 4 to 5 percent Malathion as the active ingredient, to be effective. Malathion is safe for limited use on or around kittens. It is available in liquid form, too, for use in spraying your yard for fleas, and may be purchased from a nursery. Read the label to make sure that no harmful chemicals are in with it. (See "Poisons.")

Other flea-control products work on the principle of dehydration of the insect. These claim long-lasting effectiveness, particularly in furniture and sleeping places. A new method of flea control is use of Ectoral tablets. Given to a cat at intervals, in dosage according to body weight, fleas, ticks, and lice die after biting the cat.

Life Cycle of a Flea

The eggs of a flea drop off the cat, and the larvae hatch in various places around the house. They then enter a pupa stage, from which later emerge the adult fleas who jump back aboard the cat.

Mac Gregor, owned by Mrs. David Comstock, models a sweater.

A small amount of flea powder on the back of the neck and the base of the tail, applied daily for ten days to two weeks, should rid your cat of adult fleas. Follow up with bi-weekly applications of flea powder and with the cleaning until you are sure there are no more fleas in any stage of development. Evidence of adult fleas are grains of "flea dirt" on the cat's skin and throughout the coat. This is a black, gritty-feeling substance which turns red when wet.

Flea eggs are white and too small for ordinary notice. The larvae are small, have 13 pairs of legs, and resemble a tiny centipede.

Check your cat and kittens often for signs of fleas. Severe flea infestation in a baby kitten can cause anemia, even death. Fleas can severely drain the blood supply and weaken the system of a cat or other animal of any age.

XIII

IN SICKNESS AND IN HEALTH

Many of the following ailments and diseases may be avoided by keeping your cat inside where you can observe his actions and, at the same time, cut down on his exposure to contagion.

The Coat

It is natural for a cat to be in good health. This is reflected in the prime condition of his fur and skin. One of the first signs that a cat is "off" is when he shows no interest in washing himself. The fur of a sick cat or kitten is limp, sticks together, and, in general, looks "tacky." A cat should look and act alert. If he sleeps or drowses hunched up and does not respond to your touch or voice, he does not feel well.

The Eyes

The eyes of a healthy cat have bright luster and will follow any movement. A sick cat pays little attention to anything, and his eyes have a dull, "liquid" appearance. Sometimes a sick cat will have what looks like a film covering part of each eye. This extra, or third, eyelid is termed "haw." Ordinarily, haws cover the eyes only during sleep. Their appearance is a symptom that needs looking into, unless an eye injury has caused a haw to come up for protection.

When a Cat Is "Off"

Generally, cats are healthy; if they are "off" for any length of time, there is some reason for it. Listlessness, dull eyes, tacky coat, loss of appetite, and loose bowels are symptomatic of nearly all cat ailments. A cat showing any one or any combination of these symptoms should be watched closely. Although the cause may be simple, *prompt treatment is important.*

Amateur vs. Professional Diagnoses

Amateur diagnosis can be harmful and expensive, and possibly result in the death of your cat. If your cat does not respond quickly to the suggested remedies for minor ailments, *consult your veterinarian immediately*. In good faith and ignorance, you can do great harm by treating him yourself, because so many illnesses are closely related or have similar symptoms. Your cat will have the proverbial nine lives only if you realize that the cheapest life insurance for your pet is availing yourself of your veterinarian's experience and skill promptly, whenever anything seems abnormal. (Incidentally, do not put too much faith in the belief that a cat always lands on his feet—he doesn't. Usually, but not every time.)

Modern techniques of medicine and surgery are being applied to cats to an ever-increasing extent. In the past twenty years veterinary diagnosis and treatment have advanced remarkably.

The resources available to veterinarians include ultra-violet lamp, X-ray picture, laboratory analysis, and bacteriological examination. These now supplement the stethoscope and thermometer as aids to accurate diagnosis, if necessary.

In treatment, a broad range of drugs is available. These drugs are manufactured under the same exacting conditions and to the same meticulous specifications as are those for human use.

Operations of the most delicate nature are performed, such as the setting and pinning of broken bones, Caesarian section, and other abdominal surgery, surgery of the eye and of the chest. Aseptic methods and improved anesthesia combine to increase the chances of success.

In the prevention of disease, feline enteritis vaccine has proved very reliable for many years. Advances are being made in isolating viruses that cause many other types of disease and developing vaccines to protect against them.

Choosing a Veterinarian

Your selection of a veterinarian for your cat should be guided by the reaction of you and your cat to his approach to your problem. The best skill and advice are not effective if you and your cat do not have a feeling of ease and confidence in the doctor himself. Most cats will respond better to a veterinarian who is experienced with cats, who likes and appreciates them. His handling of your cat conveys this experience and attitude, and it is reflected in your cat's behavior with him.

A Sick Cat Needs Encouragement

When a cat is sick he feels bad all over and his spirits sag. Regardless of whether your sick cat is treated at home by you or at the veterinary hospital, it is important to keep up his morale. Devoted, sympathetic care and nursing will help a sick cat recover more quickly. Sometimes it will determine whether he will recover or not. A sick cat very easily becomes discouraged, and some do not really try to get well without a great deal of encouragement and cheering up.

Hairballs

All cats swallow the loose hair that comes off when they clean themselves. The more you keep your cat combed and brushed out, the fewer hairs there are to accumulate in the digestive tract. They ball up and form a cigar-shaped wad. Many cats will vomit them or pass them in the bowel movement. If they do, there is no problem. To facilitate passage, give a weekly dosage of a teaspoonful (for an adult cat) or less (for a kitten) of salad oil, white non-carbolated vaseline, or any of the malt-flavored petrolatum products made for this purpose. Use of mineral oil is not recommended because, being non-irritating, it will not be coughed up if it goes down the wrong way. It may get down into the lungs and cause mechanical pneumonia. If a hairball does not pass and causes an obstruction of fecal material, it is necessary to try to remove it with an enema or, in extreme cases, by surgery.

Diarrhea

Simple digestive upsets evidenced by loose bowels and vomiting can be treated with remedies used for children, such as Kaopectate or milk of bismuth. These preparations have an astringent action on the intestinal mucous membranes; they considerably lessen the production of toxins and gas. Two to four teaspoonfuls,

Young kittens and puppies usually get along well together, especially if they are between 4 and 8 weeks of age. It is very difficult to adapt adult dogs and cats to be friendly if they haven't known each other in their first weeks of life. Photo by C.L.I.

depending on the size of the cat, given every two to four hours, should relieve these symptoms.

In addition to the medication, temporarily eliminate dairy products from the diet. If you suspect the upset has resulted from a change of diet, go back to the original one. In general, a diet exclusively of muscle meat will help to control the disturbance.

When the foregoing measures do not correct the problem and symptoms have persisted for more than twenty-four hours, have your veterinarian examine the cat to obtain the correct diagnosis of their cause and prescribe an effective treatment.

Non-specific, non-infectious inflammation of the digestive tract may be caused by any of the following: various resident bacteria, heavy worm infestation or repeated de-worming, chills, foreign bodies, or impacted bowels. Also, there may be an infection that has settled in the digestive tract, or the symptoms may be an early warning of a specific disease.

Liver Disorders

Cats which have loose gray extremely malodorous stools frequently prove to be afflicted with faulty fat digestion. Other symptoms are a spiky, greasy look and feel to the fur, and excessively oily skin. A cat may be thin and its general condition listless and poor, without specific symptoms. Any or all of these conditions could be an indication of faulty functioning of the liver or pancreas, or both. Treatment with oral preparations (such as Cholimeth or Hepacaps) which contain Choline, Inositol, Methionine, and B_{12}, often will result in immediate and spectacular improvement of the animal's stool, appetite, coat, appearance, and general health. Upset metabolism of the individual cat seems to be a factor to consider when a cat is not exactly sick, but is not perfectly healthy, either.

Constipation

Hard or infrequent bowel movements suggest an adjustment in the diet to produce softer stools, or a slightly more laxative effect. No evidence of any bowel movement or just a watery one—especially when accompanied by vomiting—indicates an obstruction of some kind.

Poisoning

Most chemicals are poisonous to cats. Particularly dangerous are DDT, Chlordane, and Lindane in any form, including insecticide powder or sprays. Many coal-tar derivatives, such as preparations containing carbolic acid or phenol compounds, are equally deadly. Phosphorus and lead can cause poisoning. Arsenic, usually found in weed and snail killers, can kill a cat. Read carefully the ingredients of *anything* you use that your cat could possibly come in contact with.

It has been reported that cats have been poisoned by eating the leaves of various house plants. Do not use around your house or yard preparations that contain any chemicals possibly poisonous to cats. Even though a cat might not eat it directly, he can get some on his feet and then lick it off.

Emergency treatment, should you suspect poisoning, is to induce vomiting. Use equal parts of three percent hydrogen peroxide and water, one tablespoonful at a time, repeating this dosage until the cat vomits. *Then take him to the veterinarian immediately*. Try to identify the poison. Better yet, take its labelled container to the veterinarian, if possible. This will facilitate treatment, as the antidote can be determined more quickly.

Warning: A cat's reaction to antihistamines is highly unpredictable. Do not give antihistamine or any other human preparation of that kind to your cat unless you have been specifically instructed to do so by your veterinarian. Occasionally, a cat or kitten will have an allergic reaction to any kind of injection, combination of injections, or medicine, just as a person will.

Ringworm and Other Fungus-Caused Skin Problems

Some cats have breaking-out of the skin due only to allergies. As ringworm (not a worm) and other fungal diseases also can cause this, it is vital that an *expert* diagnosis be made so that proper treatment may be undertaken at the doctor's direction as soon as possible. Different types of fungi respond to different types of medication. New methods, using drugs (such as griseofulvin) that work internally, have shown great promise for speedily eradicating ringworm. Ringworm is the only common

Blue-eyed White female owned by Don Martin: DBL. CH. GALLAHAD'S
DECIBEL. Sire: Windibank Breezi of Gallahad; dam: Milky Way's Iris of
Gallahad. Bred by Blanche Wolfram Smith. Photo by Louise Van der Meid.

Red male owned and bred by Miss Lucy Clingan: CH. KERRY LU RED PRINCE. Sire: Tr. Ch. Shanna Groith White Bugle; dam: Ch. Myowne Cream Faery of Kerry Lu. Photo by Louise Van der Meid.

Chinchilla Silver kittens owned by Adele Magill. Photo by Louise Van der Meid.

skin disease that can be transmitted to and from cats and humans. For a long-haired cat that does not receive immediate and correct attention, treatment often stretches over a long period.

Eczema

Individual cats are allergic to certain foods and, as a result, will either break out in a rash or in sores. It has been found that the presence of fleas and the use of irritating flea powders and sprays can cause severe outbreaks on the skin. Worm infestation can cause a skin reaction in some cats. Vitamin deficiency often is at fault, as well as too much vitamin supplementing. In some cases it is found to be a combination of things that cause the eczema.

The remedy is fairly obvious, once the cause has been determined, but considerable detective work may be required to track it down. If the skin reaction is severe, an anti-allergy shot may be given to relieve the symptoms. Baths with a medicated shampoo often will soothe and help clear up skin inflammation.

Swellings

Swelling in any part of the body indicates injury or infection. Bear in mind that a cat's skin heals very readily and that a scratch or bite wound may seal over quickly on top; outwardly, the skin shows no break, while infection runs rampant beneath the skin and throughout the system. Treatment, after lancing and antibiotic injections, consists primarily in keeping the scab removed, as the wound must be kept open to heal from the inside.

Teeth

A cat with a sore mouth doesn't want to chew or eat. Teeth should be checked for tartar accumulations. When tartar is present, the teeth should be scaled to prevent irritation of the gums and the possibility of infection. Any infected teeth should be removed. Infection from abscessed teeth or roots could spread throughout a cat's entire system.

Teething

Between the ages of four and seven months, kittens lose their baby teeth and cut a permanent set. This often is the reason a kitten seems hungry yet does not eat. Check his mouth. Sometimes, when a tooth is just barely attached, you can help by removing it. If his mouth is sore, he will not want to chew, so offer him soft or liquid food at this time.

Teething frequently is accompanied by sore gums, bowel upsets, and varying degrees of fever, all of which contribute to the lack of appetite. Treatment with antibiotics is indicated in some cases when a kitten's whole system is thrown off by his teething. Occasionally some baby teeth are retained, with the permanent ones coming in alongside them. If this condition persists, the baby teeth should be extracted by a veterinarian.

Cystitis

The urinary bladder normally is situated in the rear of the abdominal cavity, but when greatly distended it protrudes well into the abdomen. This distention is a symptom of cystitis, a condition in which the cat is unable to pass his urine. To the touch, the bladder will feel as large and as hard as an orange. A cat with a full bladder acts anxious, uneasy, and restless, and has little appetite. He tries unsuccessfully to urinate at frequent intervals, perhaps passing just a few drops. Often he shows a complete disregard for his usual clean toilet habits. The condition is extremely painful, and he may cry plaintively, growl, or bite when touched or picked up.

This is a definite emergency. Unless the urine is expelled and the bladder relieved of this pressure as soon as possible, it will cause uremic poisoning, resulting in his death in a very short time.

If your cat goes to the pan frequently and strains, seeming to eliminate only a small amount of urine painfully, see about it immediately. This symptom of straining at urination is commonly mistaken as constipation. Also, keep a close watch on a cat that suddenly takes to urinating in strange places.

One cause of stoppage is the formation in the bladder of

Kittens love to play among the blooming spring plants; they often find "weeds" which they eat (like catnip). Photo by C.L.I.

Cream male owned by Mrs. Betty Meins: DBL. CH. ZODA'S ROSE PAR-ADE OF LA CRESTA. Sire: Frivolous of Pensford (Imp.); dam: Zoda's Honeycomb. Bred by Zoe McEachern. Photo by Louise Van der Meid.

material like grains of fine sand. These granules pack together and lodge in the small urethral passage, thereby plugging the outlet. To open this, the veterinarian can sometimes pass a catheter which enables him to draw off the urine and then attempt to flush out the bladder and inject medicine. In more extreme situations, surgery is required to accomplish these vital steps. Often it is necessary to continue expelling the urine manually and to repeat the catheterization, since the bladder muscle becomes paralyzed from strain and cannot function, even though the opening has been cleared. Drugs are used to restore bladder tone and acidify the urine, which help to prevent further formation of sand. Special low-ash diets are prescribed. A tendency toward formation of bladder sand seems to be inheritable. No specific cause of this condition has ever been found.

Another condition producing similar symptoms is that of a mucus, or pus, plug. Often blood is present in the urine. This condition sometimes has a high temperature symptom, and is due to an infection or irritation in the bladder or urethra. Irritation may be caused by unsuccessful breeding attempts or too frequent breeding. If infection is present, antibiotics or sulfa drugs are given, in addition to the other treatment given after the passage is opened.

In the female cat, the passage, being larger, seldom closes entirely, and there is not the extreme emergency present, as in the case of the male. However, females can get cystitis (inflammation of the bladder). It can become serious in a female due to its debilitating effect. Occasionally, there will be the same emergency problem as with males, due to their being unable to pass enough urine normally.

Regular or buffered aspirin, given in doses of one-half tablet every three hours, may help relax the congested area and make the cat more comfortable until he can be taken to the veterinarian.

It is sometimes necessary to resort to surgery in chronic, severe cases of cystitis, to create a new opening for the passage of urine. This operation more often than not is successful, but nevertheless causes some inconvenience, for obvious reasons, during and after convalescence.

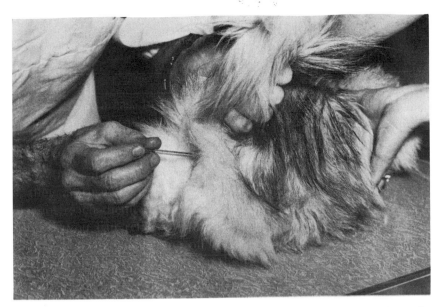

Gently insert the thermometer, after first lubricating its tip, into the cat's anus. Photo by Louise Van der Meid.

Fever

The normal rectal temperature of a cat is 101 to 102 degrees. Without a thermometer, you can detect fever by holding your hand across the ears and face. Paw-pads, too, will feel burning to the touch. Excitement can cause slight fever. Occasionally, when a kitten is cutting its permanent teeth, at from four to seven months of age, it will have "teething fever." It may run a high temperature, and it may not eat, because of sore gums. Usually, however, fever indicates an infection of some kind and, as such, requires diagnosis and treatment by a veterinarian. One-half of a five-grain aspirin tablet given at three- to four-hour intervals can relieve fever or pain until the cat can be examined.

Convulsions

Like fever, convulsions are symptoms, rather than a disease, and may result from a number of causes. Do not attempt any treatment until you consult a veterinarian for his diagnosis and remedy.

107

Shaded Silver male owned and bred by Dr. and Mrs. P. N. Ramsdale: DEAR-HEART SIR WINSTON. Sire: Dbl. Ch. Mr. Rhett Butler; dam: Reene's Marie of Dearheart. Photo by Don Martin.

It is almost as much trouble to take care of two cats as one!

Anemia

Severe anemia, or lack of red blood corpuscles or hemoglobin, or both, may be detected by looking at a cat's gums and tongue. If they are pale the cat is anemic and needs to be treated. Have a veterinarian check the cat to determine the cause of the condition and prescribe treatment. Anemia may have simple or complex origins, and must be treated accordingly. We find that a liver and iron tonic, with B-complex and B_{12} vitamins added, is effective in preventing cases of anemia in nursing mothers and picking up a fussy appetite which might stem from a slight anemia.

Parasites

General poor condition, lack-luster coat, light weight (even though the appetite is good), chronic loose bowels or bloody stool, and, in some cases, an allergic skin reaction, each—or all —may be symptoms of parasitic infection. The most common are tapeworms, roundworms, and coccidiosis.

Tapeworms

Tapeworm segments, similar in appearance to grains of rice, are eliminated in the stool and can be detected there, or will be observed sticking to the fur around the anus. De-worming should be done by a veterinarian. If the powerful medicine necessary to kill the tapeworm does not pass through the cat's system in a very short time, it must be removed by an enema, as it would poison the cat if allowed to remain in its system. Repeated treatment at two- to three-week intervals may be necessary to clear up severe cases of infestation. Tapeworms will grow again if their extremely small "heads" are not dislodged from the cat's intestinal wall by de-worming.

The connection between the presence of fleas and the tapeworm cycle is as follows: the flea eats the tapeworm egg which is inside the segment passed out by the cat, and the egg hatches inside the flea and completes its larval development there. If the cat should swallow a dead or live flea with these potential tapeworms in it, he, in turn, becomes host to the adult tapeworm.

Fleas must be eliminated to assure no more tapeworms, once the existing ones are eliminated. If fleas cannot be eliminated entirely, keeping their number to a minimum will lessen the chance of tapeworm reinfestation. Flea control is described fully in the section on caring for a Persian's coat.

There are other types of tapeworms in cats which have different intermediate hosts for their eggs, such as mice and fish. Although these are more rare, treatment is the same.

Roundworms

The presence of roundworms may be found by laboratory analysis of fecal matter. Sometimes these wiry, spaghetti-like worms may be vomited. Ascarids, or roundworms, do not require an intermediate host. The larval stages of the roundworm's development take place within the cat, the adult roundworms laying their eggs in his intestines, to be passed out in his feces and contaminate the ground.

From the ground, this same cat (and others) gets these eggs on feet or fur; when he washes, the eggs get into his digestive tract. The roundworm larva hatches in the cat's intestine and burrows into the intestinal wall. It then gets into the bloodstream and is carried to the liver, where it is usually filtered out of the blood. The larva then starts migrating into the surrounding tissue.

If it migrates to the lungs, it completes its larval development in the air passages of the lungs, works its way up toward the mouth, and is coughed up and swallowed. Upon reaching the intestine again, it becomes an adult worm and starts reproducing.

Not all larvae reach the lungs in their migration; some may wander aimlessly in the abdominal cavity for a while and then become dormant. In the case of the female cat, pregnancy seems to activate these migratory larvae. The larvae may migrate into the uterus and into the embryonic kittens. They go through the rest of their cycle within the kitten, causing the kitten to be infested with roundworms at birth. This explains why many litters of kittens may be found to have roundworms when there is no known history of roundworms in the mother.

Fecal examination, the usual method of detecting the presence of roundworms, shows only that adult egg-laying worms are pre-

Coccidiosis, with a bloody diarrhea symptom, is easily transmitted from cat to cat. If you have a sick kitten (or cat), isolate her from your other pets. Photo by C.L.I.

sent in the intestines; if they are not in this stage of their cycle, they cannot be diagnosed.

Roundworms, if present, are usually removed by the same medicine used for the removal of tapeworms. This procedure is not always advisable in the case of small kittens, however.

To treat only roundworms, piperazine compounds in recommended dosages may be given directly or mixed with the food. These are very effective against the adult roundworm, but are not effective against tapeworm or any roundworm larvae or eggs. Repeated treatment at weekly intervals is necessary to rid a cat of roundworms.

Coccidiosis

This parasitic infection is caused by a protozoan organism which lives within the cells lining the small intestine. As these complete their cycle and the eggs, or oocysts, become ready, the intestinal cell ruptures, allowing their release. In the early stages of infection there may be a severe systematic reaction and fever. Diarrhea usually occurs intermittently. If the infection is not too extensive and has been present long enough for the cat to build up some resistance, there may be no symptoms. Diagnosis can be made only by fecal examination. Both diagnosis and treatment should be done by a veterinarian. Consistent bloody diarrhea may be caused by coccidiosis, particularly in young cats or kittens. Transmission to other cats is common and likely. Usually, it is passed on by the washing of feet or fur contaminated by contact with the feces of an already infected cat.

Earmites

Mites themselves, tiny and white, are not apparent to the naked eye. The irritation of the ear canal caused by their presence produces a brown or black crumbly wax in and about the ears. Scratching the ears and shaking the head indicate the possibility of infestation. Earmites are extremely contagious from, and to, other cats and animals, although not to people. Persistent treatment with an effective product can clear up the condition, once it is discovered. The mites, too, have a cycle of reproduction, and the eggs must hatch to be killed by the medicine. Little

114

is effective in killing any kind of insect eggs. There may be secondary infection in the ears that will need further treatment.

Ticks

Ticks are found in some areas. In cattle-raising country, the spinose ear tick may get into a cat's ears—if he goes in the areas where cattle graze. This type of tick should be removed by a veterinarian.

Other species of ticks attach themselves to the skin of an animal. In cats, they are usually found on the head and neck, where the cat cannot reach them. If the head of the tick is not too deeply imbedded, you can remove it by gently pulling on the body of the tick. If it does not come off readily, sprinkle a little flea powder or a drop of spray directly on the tick. In a few hours the tick will die and drop off whole, by itself.

Maggots

Be very careful that flies cannot get to a long-haired cat that is not feeling well. If a cat is sick, or will not or cannot wash himself for any reason, he may become flyblown. Also, flies will be attracted by any bloody discharge or sore or to a cat that has diarrhea. If the eggs are laid and not cleaned off, they hatch into maggots. These maggots will eat right into a cat's flesh in a very short time. Their action quickly produces a toxic reaction in the cat's system, and extreme weakness and death soon follow.

If such a condition is discovered, dose the spot or spots heavily with flea powder immediately. This will help slow down the maggots on the outside, at least. Then *rush* to the veterinarian to have the rest removed as quickly as possible. Minutes sometimes count. There are very few things which could be used to kill the maggots inside without also further injury to the cat, so they have to be removed by hand or probe.

This is a horrifying experience, one you need never have, if aware of the possibility.

In some areas there are flies, such as botflies and screw worm flies, which will lay eggs on an animal's coat, particularly if

Chinchilla Silver female owned and bred by Mr. and Mrs. E. W. Peterson: QUAD. GR. CH. BEVERLY-SERRANO PETITE. Sire: Gr. Ch. Beverly-Serrano Keo; dam: Tr. Ch. Joy of Beverly-Serrano. Photo by Louise Van der Meid.

Smoke male owned by Mr. and Mrs. Paul Raine: CH. UWAHI NUI NUI OF FAIR OAKS. Sire: Ch. Nuikane Rania of Spring Mountain; dam: Spring Mountain Cinderella. Bred by Winifred Miles. Photo by Louise Van der Meid.

Do not give a lovely longhair to anyone who will not take care of it properly. Too often kittens are given for Christmas presents without the giver inquiring into the acceptability of a "live" gift. Photo by C.L.I.

it is the least bit damp. These eggs hatch almost immediately, and the maggots burrow into the flesh in a matter of hours, with the same tragic results.

Insect Bites

Bites from spiders, ants, and other pests produce a severe reaction in some cats. When a cat is bitten near the eye, swelling can cause the third eyelid, or "haw," to come up and sometimes completely cover the eye. Other mysterious swellings of the face or paws also may be due to insect bite reactions. They usually subside in a day or two, but may require anti-allergy treatment, if the swelling is in a place which would cause interference with the cat's breathing or swallowing.

Viral Diseases and Vaccinations

There are many types of viruses and germs which can cause any number of diseases, but these are more or less rare occurrences in cats, with the following exceptions:

Rabies

Although any warm-blooded animal can contract rabies, cats are not usually vaccinated against it—unless there is an epidemic in the area. It is required for certain interstate or foreign shipments.

Feline Enteritis

Sometimes there is a confusion or misunderstanding when the word "enteritis" is used. Enteritis, or inflammation of the cat's intestinal tract, is a general diagnosis when this is the case, from whatever cause. There is also a specific deadly disease in cats, properly called *infectious feline panleucopenia*, commonly referred to as feline enteritis, feline distemper, or cat fever. There is an excellent vaccine which gives protection against this cat killer, Recommended age for vaccination is eight to nine weeks. Young cats are particularly susceptible, although cats of any age can contract it. Booster shots may be given as a further precaution every one or two years; if there is an outbreak in your neighborhood, shots can be given more often.

Onset of the disease is characterized by listnessness, weakness, vomiting of a yellowish fluid, diarrhea showing the same type of fluid, fever, and hanging of the head over a water dish. If an unvaccinated cat shows these symptoms, *rush it to the veterinarian for serum and supporting treatment.* The course to death from feline enteritis often is so swift that it is mistaken for poisoning.

The virus is passed by contact, either directly or indirectly, with areas contaminated by an infected cat. The disease is very infectious, but to members of the cat family only, not to dogs or people. It is not safe to bring an unvaccinated cat into any place where cat fever has been until at least six months have passed.

For further protection, a booster shot may be given each year after the initial vaccination.

Pneumonitis and other Respiratory Infections

Symptoms of these diseases resemble the symptoms of a severe cold in a human. The eyes water, the nose runs, the throat is sore, and the sufferer coughs and sneezes and seems to be sore all over. He is sometimes feverish, listless, and will not eat. Sometimes the bowels are loose. Treatment in the early stages gives the best and quickest results.

When a cat shows any of these symptoms, isolate him immediately, and isolate all cats with which he may have been in contact. These diseases are spread through the air and through contact with articles that have been sneezed or coughed upon.

Some of the respiratory infections are not as serious as pneumonitis, but as the early symptoms and treatment are identical, it is best to presume such an illness to be pneumonitis, and institute treatment accordingly. If it is merely a rhinitis or coryza condition, it will clear up fairly easily with treatment, and you and your cat are fortunate.

Pneumonitis can be a killer, although its course is not as rapid as cat fever.

When a cat's nose is stopped up, he cannot smell his food and will not care to eat. In addition, if his throat is sore, it hurts him to swallow. The pneumonitis virus attacks the mucous membranes, inflames the eyes, nose, throat, and intestines, and goes

The difference between a potential champion and an ordinary long-hair is only the initial investment. It costs the same to care for a "show" kitten as a "pet" quality kitten, but its pedigree has little to do with its pet qualities. Photo by C.L.I.

Blue male owned and bred by Mary Ann Maxwell: CH. BRE-ETTA PER-FECTO. Sire: Azulita Personality of Bre-Etta; dam: Azulita Parizata of Bre-Etta. Photo by Louise Van der Meid.

Tortoiseshell female owned and bred by Mrs. Dottie Woods: CH. AZURE'S KISMET. Sire: Tr. Ch. Angelita's King Cole; dam: Ch. Shawnee Cardinalette. Photo by Louise Van der Meid.

down into the lungs. The virus itself can be held somewhat in check by antibiotic treatment, but in the patient's refusal to eat, which accompanies the infection, there is an extremely dangerous weakening effect. Force feeding often must be resorted to, or, in extreme cases, feeding via an infant's nasal-feeding tube by a veterinarian.

The problem has been to find a food which will provide enough calories per volume, yet avoid diarrhea. One product that has been found satisfactory is Borden's Liquid Mullsoy. This condensed soy bean milk, if fortified with vitamins, seems to sustain life and give the medicine a chance to do its work in controlling both the virus and secondary infections. Other factors important in the treatment of pneumonitis are a continuous warm, even temperature, with *no drafts*, and good nursing.

Several strains of pneumonitis virus which cause similar symptoms have been isolated, and vaccinations have been developed against some of the more common ones.

Although vaccination is an excellent precaution, immunity doesn't last long, and vaccination has to be repeated periodically. A recovered cat can have recurrences. He may be a carrier with few or no symptoms of chronic infection, and infect other cats with which he comes in contact. The other cats can get the disease in severe form without any suspicion of exposure.

Particularly susceptible to the virus are kittens at weaning age and cats or kittens whose resistance has been lowered. Dogs and humans are not susceptible to these feline respiratory viruses.

How to Give a Pill or Capsule

If you are right-handed, grasp the cat's head with the left hand, place your thumb under the bony ridge under and behind the cat's right eye, and place the first two or three fingers under the corresponding ridge under the left eye. Crook your little finger back into the palm so that it rests just behind the cat's head, thus establishing a firmer hold.

Take the pill or capsule between the thumb and forefinger of the right hand and with the middle finger insert the finger-nail between the upper and lower front teeth, pushing down on the lower teeth. At the same time, tip the cat's head upward with the left hand. This will help to open the cat's mouth, as well as get your right hand farther from his front claws. When a cat's mouth is wide open, it will be noticed that a groove forms at the base of the tongue. Drop the pill or capsule down into this groove, pushing it down quickly over the base of the tongue with the right index finger (or the eraser end of a pencil, if necessary). Then quickly close the cat's mouth, sliding the left thumb around under the cat's lower jaw to hold it closed. Then, to encourage swallowing, massage from the chin back and down toward the throat with the fingers of the right hand.

With some cats, it is helpful to have another person hold the front feet down. Coating the pill or capsule with butter will lubricate it and speed up the ordeal for both you and the cat. The more quickly and deftly the pill is given, the better the chances of success on the first try.

Use your index finger to push the pill or capsule down the cat's throat, hold his mouth shut, and then rub his throat to make him swallow. A little butter on the medication often makes it go down easier. Photo by Louise Van der Meid.

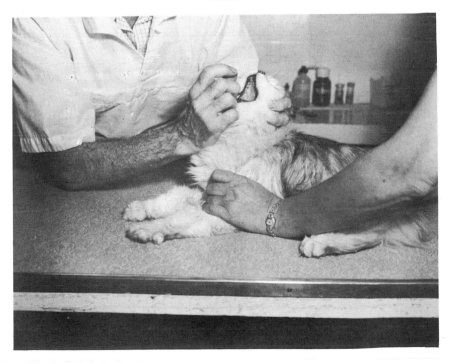

Silver Tabby female owned and bred by Mrs. Don Martin: DBL. CH. SILVER SWORD'S FILIGREE. Sire: Tr. Ch. Sir Pepper of Silver Vista; dam: Tr. Ch. Marleon Fur Fun Merrilegs. Photo by Louise Van der Meid.

Red Tabby male owned by Mrs. Helen Smith: DBL. CH. SPERO STINK-PUFF OF SMITHWAY. Sire: Spero Count de Stripes; dam: Spero Royale Flush. Bred by Mr. and Mrs. Carl Johnson. Photo by Louise Van der Meid.

Shell Cameo male **PACO TICO ADONNIS OF ELEGANTE,** owned by Velma Echeverria, bred by Kathleen Simkins. Sire: Elegante Silver Feather; dam: Pixie of Paco Tico.

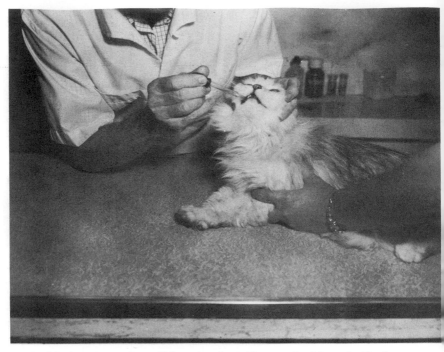

Liquid vitamins and medicines are best dispensed with a plastic dropper.
Photo by Louise Van der Meid.

How to Give Liquid Medication

The easiest way to give most cats liquid medicine is to use a plastic medicine dropper. If he bites down on it, a glass one might break. Put the dropper in the side of his mouth to avoid choking him. If it is necessary to force him to open his mouth, follow the procedure for giving a pill. Some cats will be agreeable to your using a teaspoon for pouring it in. To avoid spilling, fill the teaspoon only half full. Cats seldom will drink milk or water that has anything added to it.

XIV

FORMAL, OR SHOW, STANDARDS FOR LONGHAIRS

HEAD: Massive and round, with great breadth of skull; jaws broad and powerful, with cheeks full and prominent. The short, snub nose should be almost as broad as long, with slight stop, or "break," between the eyes. In Peke-face varieties, the head should resemble as much as possible the Pekingese dog from which the name is derived. The nose should be very short and indented between the eyes. The muzzle should be decidedly wrinkled.

Objections: Long, narrow head; long, Roman or humped nose; thin muzzle; overshot or undershot jaw; irregularities of the teeth.

EARS: Small, round-tipped, set wide apart and not unduly open at the base, pricked forward as though listening.

Objections: Large, pointed ears; ears slanting out from the head, or set too close together.

EYES: The openings should be large and round, with the eyes brilliant and set far apart, giving a sweet expression to the face. Their color should conform to the requirements for the coat color.

Objections: Small eyes; eyes set on a bias or close together.

BODY: Short, level back and a well-rounded mid-section. The neck should be short and powerful, providing adequate support for the massive head. Chest broad and deep.

Objections: Narrow or indented chest; long, narrow back; slab flanks; long or thin neck; light bone structure.

LEGS: Short, thick and heavy-boned; forelegs should be perfectly straight. The feet should be large, round, and firm, with toes close together; five toes on front feet and four on hind feet.

Objections: Long legs; bow legs; oval feet and separated toes. Extra toes disqualify.

Large dogs often accept kittens into their "home" especially if the kitten is small and hasn't learned to fear dogs. Photo by C.L.I.

TAIL: Short; carried without a curve, at an angle lower than the back, but it should not trail when cat is walking.

Objections: Long tail; kinked tail.

COAT: Primarily, coat should reflect cat's perfect physical condition. It should be of a fine, soft texture, appear glossy and full of life, and should stand off from the body. The coat should be long all over the body, including at the shoulders. The ruff should be immense and continue in a deep frill between the front legs. Ear tufts should be long and curved; toe tufts should be long. The tail should be very full (like a fox's brush).

The cat should be firm in flesh, but not fat, well-balanced physically and temperamentally, gentle and amenable to handling.

GENERAL APPEARANCE: Medium to large, but with no sacrifice of quality for the sake of mere size; heavy-boned; short-coupled; cobby; the whole giving the impression of robust power.

COLOR: For the recognized colors and color patterns, see the color plates and descriptions. Points for cats with special markings should be divided between color and markings.

Objections: Any cat whose coloring differs markedly from the recognized proper shade or pattern shall be penalized or, in some cases, transferred to the Any-Other-Color Class, which does not have Championship Awards.

The Cat Fanciers' Association judges' scoring for Longhairs:

	Points
Color	20
Coat	10
Condition	10
Head (including size and shape of eyes)... ...	30
Body type (including shape, size, bone structure and tail length)	20
Color of eyes	10
Total ...	100

Some of the terms used in the standard, such as short, wide, cobby, etc., make the perfection of these qualities a little hard for the novice to picture. Perhaps it might be better explained in less technical terms, as in the following paragraphs.

Type and Proportion of Persians

The most desirable face and body type for a Persian are parts that are in proper proportion to the whole and to each other, the whole presenting a nearly square, or cobby, appearance. This basic square should be softly rounded off to avoid a severe impression. A nose that would be considered long if it were on one cat is not too long on one having a larger, wider head. The same applies to legs, tails, bodies, and all other features.

In like manner, an extremely short tail would not make a pleasant finish to a large cat, whereas it might look fine on a small one. Balance is another word that means proportion, but, specifically, it may have to do with the weight distribution. A Persian should not be so extra heavy on either end that the other end suffers by comparison.

Head

The ideal head of a Persian cat could be divided into equal sections. The distances from forehead top to nose and from nose to chin bottom should be the same. The upcurving mouth, muzzle and chin, with the jaw bone as wide as the top of the head, helps give the desired "sweet expression." The nose should be flat and as broad at the tip as it is at the base, with a definite "break," or stop, where it meets the forehead. The distance between the eyes should be the width of the eye itself, or more, and the nose

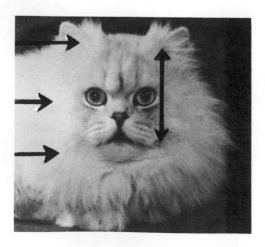

The three arrows at the left of this photo illustrate the correct alignment of features: the distance from the top of the nose to the top of the skull is equal to that between the top of the nose and the bottom of the chin. The arrow on the right indicates the proper alignment of the ear with the outer corner of the eye.

This view illustrates the wide snub nose (with definite stop, or "break"), forward pricked ears, and sweet, smiling facial expression.

length should be this same distance, or shorter. The ears should be set even with the corners of the eyes and should not be of a size or length that would make them appear to be appendages rather than part of the head. The ears should be neither wide nor open at the base.

Body

The actual features of the cat are sometimes covered by the fur which is the window-dressing of a Persian. Judges smooth back the fur to find the structure of the cat underneath. It has been said that you should have a well-built house before you try to paint it. A Persian cat should have Persian "type," regardless of coat or color. Even when it is clipped or wringing wet you should still be able to see that it *is* a Persian. The body should be short and wide, well-muscled, the chest broad and well developed, with no impression of shallowness. Legs, short and broad; feet, large but firmly muscled, not splayed. The neck should be short and broad, joining the head and body in a beautiful curve. A Persian's tail is properly short and bushy, the same width from tip to base. The whole cat should have a substantial feel, heavy and chunky, but not overly fat; the bones themselves should be heavy. If the Siamese may be compared to a thoroughbred race horse, the Persian may be compared to a Clydesdale or a Percheron draft horse. In discussing breeding possibilities for the various colors, all these things are included when the word "type" is used.

XV

RECOGNIZED COLORS OF LONGHAIRS

Color Divisions for Show Cats

In the United States at the present time, Persian, or purebred long-haired cats, are classified in three divisions for show purposes. Hybrid Longhairs have a separate division.

Those cats whose coats are unmarked and are all of one color are called Solid Colors or Self-Colors. This includes White, Black, Blue, Cream, Red, and Peke-Face Reds. They comprise the Solid Color Division.

Patched cats, whose coats are combinations of two or more of these solid colors, are the Blue Creams, Tortoiseshells, and Calicos (or Tortie with White). These are grouped with the vari-colored Tabby-marked cats, Brown, Blue, Red, Peke-Face Red Tabbies and (usually) Silver Tabbies, to make up the Tabby and Tortoiseshell Division.

The Silver Division includes Chinchilla Silvers, Shaded Silvers, Blue and Black Smokes, the Tabby, Cameo Colors (Shell, Shaded, and Smoke), and sometimes Silver Tabbies. Some associations have a separate division for Cameos.

The Silver Tabbies can fit in the Silver category, but are also Tabbies. As their tabbiness is more distinctive than their silveriness, they are usually included in the Tabby and Tortoiseshell Division.

Evolution of Colors and Type

All colors of the present day purebred longhair, or Persian, probably were produced by selective breeding of the original Angoras, now extinct, and their mixture with the also-called "Persians" originating in Afghanistan. Although the common ancestor of all cats was, no doubt, speckled or striped, this original Angora, from Ankara, Turkey, was almost certainly a white cat, or white with only a small amount of coloration. (A white coat is not necessarily the result of the absence of color, as is the case when the animal is an albino. Albinism in cats is very rare.) The Angora cat imported from the Far East may really have been carrying genetically all colors of coat under a white mask.

As time progressed and nature intervened, various colored kittens appeared in the litters and Angoras later came in all colors, including Tabbies. As stated previously, those that were the most prevalent and popular in England were blue (or Maltese) sometimes with white markings. Other colors that breeders thought were attractive were developed by selective color breeding. Definite families of cats having the same coloring began to be established by breeding like to like.

The Persians, too, came in a variety of colors, but darkly marked Tabbies and Tortoiseshells were quite rare. When, of necessity, the two longhair strains began to be blended, those who wished to develop the Tabbies had to keep more of the Angora tendencies (longer body, pointed face, and larger, pointed ears). In order to keep and improve certain patterns and markings they wanted in Tabbies, it was necessary for them to breed Tabby to Tabby. These characteristics of the original Angora type were unable to be offset by breeding to a Tabby "Persian," as there were so few of them at that time.

This same background, slightly more predominantly Angora, may also be present behind the Silvers. They probably originated from lightly-marked Silver Tabbies. Silver, too, was a comparatively rare color in Tabbies. Although Silvers first appeared as a new color in the early 1900's, unfortunately their background and early breeding developments were not recorded.

The Tortoiseshell coloring—black, cream, and red, which also was rare in the old-time Persian—is sex-linked, so practically all Torties are females. (Occasionally a male will appear, but males usually are sterile.) Inasmuch as females could be bred to males of any color, the "Persian type" was more easily introduced in Torties than in Tabbies.

Over the years, however, all the colors of the longhairs have been bred to become more in keeping with the desired Persian type. The Blues conform to the standard to the most consistent degree, as they have been bred and "fancied" in greater numbers over a long period of time. Breeders are constantly working to improve the other colors, and, through careful breeding programs, many individual cats of all color varieties now compare with the Blues for type.

Breeding Programs

There are certain definite genetic rules governing the inheritance of specific characteristics for all species. It is difficult, however, to apply these rules with significant results to the breeding of longhairs. Their offspring are not produced in sufficient numbers to demonstrate any conclusive pattern. We do make use of them, but only in a general way, because each cat has its own pattern of dominance and recessiveness, together with many modifying factors.

For example, a general rule is that yellow or copper is dominant over green or blue eye color. However, if a green-eyed male from a genetically strong green-eyed background is mated to a copper-eyed female from a genetically weak eye-color strain, *his green* may predominate over *her copper* to produce green-eyed kittens.

Prepotency, according to Professor Jay L. Lush, professor of animal breeding, Iowa State College, is the ability of a parent to carry on or to impress its characteristics on its own progeny with greater uniformity than the average parent can.

Prepotencies are more easily discerned in the male for the statistical reason that in a year's time a male may sire many litters while a female produces only one or two litters. Only after it has been determined that an individual seems to be prepotent for certain characteristics do we have a basis from which to work toward any desired end in either color or type.

The foregoing conclusions are valid only insofar as any one individual cat is concerned; thus the same procedure has to be followed to determine the potential for each cat included in a breeding program. These circumstances put the breeding of longhaired cats closer to the category of an art than that of an exact science.

Linebreeding

Linebreeding refers to the mating of cats which are related to one ancestor. Cousins, uncles, and grandfathers (or other relatives that have some common ancestors and also some unrelated cats in their pedigrees) may be considered for modified linebreeding. Inbred-linebred cats result from brother-to-sister matings. Inbreeding is employed to set certain wanted characteristics. Unfortunately, unwanted features are, also, set the same way. Mating father to daughter and then continuing to mate back to this same male is close linebreeding, serving the same purpose as inbreeding. No type of close breeding should be practiced to any degree by the novice. Persons who do so should be fully aware of the possibilities and qualities of the cats involved, and have a plan or purpose in mind.

Outcrossing is mating two cats who are related not at all, or only to a very slight degree, in an attempt to achieve improvement of specific features. The result of outcrossing is largely a matter of luck, as no one has knowledge of how any two lines will combine until he tries it. Linebreeding does give more of a family-trend type of picture from which to predict the results, and, in a modified form, is the type of breeding most generally favored.

Copper-Eyed White female owned by Mrs. Walker Johnston: DBL. GR. and QUAD. CH. WINDIBANK PATTIKAKE OF AZULITA, 1961 CAT OF YEAR OPPOSITE SEX. Sire: Ch. Dixieland Dilli of Windibank; dam: Ch. June Rose Bear of Dunesk (Imp). Bred by Mrs. F. L. Tebbetts.

XVI
WHITE PERSIANS

The White Persian of today may have any one of three types of eye color: Blue, Copper, or Odd-Eye (one eye blue, the other copper). This is the only color Persian that is permitted a variety of eye color. Each group is judged separately at the shows, then Best White of all eye colors is picked as an additional win.

Any white coat is difficult to keep in immaculate condition, and is achieved only by careful attention to grooming and bathing in order to avoid any tinge of yellow spoiling the clean bright whiteness. Any trace of grease in the fur or on the skin will combine with dirt from the air to dull its beauty. The tail and feet are most inclined to have this tendency. Also, saliva can discolor places that are licked.

Copper-Eyed White male: CH. TOIREH TYRONE OF GRAY IVY. Sire: Gr. Ch. Toireh Precious Le Noir; dam: Ch. Toireh Octavia. Breeder: Celia Herlot.

Blue-Eyed White

Many persons do not know that Persians come in a wide variety of colors. When they think of a Persian (or Angora), they usually picture a Blue-eyed White cat with long hair. The beauty of the pure white coat is set off by bright sapphire blue eyes, pink-lined ears, pink nose, mouth, and toe pads. Added to this beauty is the wide-eyed innocent expression that has always made them a favorite with the general public.

However, breeders of Blue-Eyed Whites have had many problems to retain and intensify the blue eye-color and at the same time improve the general style or type of these Persians. In addition, there is their tendency to be wholly or partially deaf. All of this results in fewer Blue-Eyed Whites being bred and shown than was the case years ago. To overcome these problems, Blue-Eyed White cats were crossed with some other color, such as Blue, or a Black with Blues in the background. As these other Persians all have copper eye color, this produced the CE, or Cop-

Blue-Eyed White male bred and owned by Mrs. Francine Puckett: FRANCINE ROBERT. Sire: Gr. Ch. Azulita Picasso of Francine; dam: Quad. Ch. Gallahad Colette of Francine.

Blue-Eyed White male owned by Mrs. Earl Fleming: GR. CH. TWINKLING STAR OF EVERGREEN. Sire: Purr-Zahn's Pearl Harbor Swami; dam: Joan of Arc II. Bred by Billy West.

per-Eyed, and the OE, or Odd-Eyed Whites.

Specific information on the probable results of various breeding procedures to produce Blue-Eyed Whites follows. These conclusions are from May Fleming of Evergreen Cattery, a well-known breeder of Blue-Eyed Whites.

Blue-Eyed Whites Bred to:

Blue-Eyed Whites: Produce the dark, sapphire blue eye color; however, loses type. Continuous breeding back to Blue-Eyed White tends to cause a reversion to longer noses, bigger ears, and more deafness.

Copper-Eyed Whites: Tend to produce copper eyes and odd eyes. Breeding to deep Copper-Eyed Whites weakens the blue eye color to gray or almost white. This bad trait has a tendency to be inherited into the third and fourth generations.

Blues: Blues are the most valuable when they carry the white gene. They must be of exceptional type, with the ability to reproduce their likeness in the offspring. From this breeding, the kittens will be Blue, Odd-Eyed White, Copper-Eyed White, and Blue-Eyed White. The Odd-Eyed female from this breeding is the most valuable for Blue-Eyed Whites, when bred back to a Blue-Eyed White sire or grandsire.

Odd-Eyed Whites: This color is the most valuable for Blue-Eyed White breeding. Many of the kittens will be blue-eyed and of sound hearing.

Blacks: Black, if color bred, is undesirable. A Black out of Blue tends to have more type, and some breeders think that Black tends to "whiten" the White.

Reds: Undesirable; lessens type and gives the coat a yellowish tinge. It is not a clear white.

Creams: Undesirable for Blue-Eyed Whites, but some breeders have had success using Creams for breeding Copper-Eyed Whites.

Silvers: Undesirable; lessens type. Offspring are dark Silvers or very poor type Blue-Eyed Whites. Good type from this breeding, while not impossible, is a rarity.

Additional suggestions from Blanche Wolfram Smith, of Gallahad Cattery, include that, in her experience, Odd Eyes may be mated to Odd Eyes, resulting in good Blue eye color. She has found that if one is proceeding for Copper-Eyed Whites, the Odd Eyes should be mated to Copper-Eyed Whites or Blue Persians. Occasionally, a Blue-Eyed White results from such a mating, but this is not likely to occur.

In general, any blue eye color tends to get lighter and fade as the adult cat grows older. In a kitten, however, the eye color may improve very noticeably to a much deeper shade of blue as the kitten matures. There should be real depth of color when the cat is fully developed. If very pale at two months of age, it probably never will change for the better, so, at that age, select the kitten with eyes of the deepest color.

The common belief that the Blue-Eyed White kitten which is born with a black or blue spot seldom, if ever, is deaf is a fallacy. Cats can carry the recessive gene for deafness, although they themselves may not be deaf. The deafness can appear in their kittens if they are mated to another Blue-Eyed White that is carrying this same gene.

The blotches of dark color are almost always gone by the time the kitten reaches one year. They are rather startling to someone who doesn't know of this phenomenon, for they sometimes appear as a large cap on the head.

The color-bred Blue-Eyed Whites tend to have small litters of kittens.

Odd-Eyed White

A White cat with Odd Eyes is an arresting sight. Most desired is for the eye that is blue to be a deep blue, or sapphire, and the other a dark orange or copper. This contrast alone makes a beautiful cat and constitutes a valuable breeding link. It is often a well-represented color class in our shows, although Odd-Eyed Whites are not eligible in England. Some Odd-Eyed Whites do not have perfect hearing, but they are seldom completely deaf.

Odd-Eyed White female owned by Suzanne Barberio: SHAH-AN-SHAH BE'L-AKHANEH. Sire: RM Quad Ch. Gallabad's Azhar; dam: Shah-An-Shah Mu Jehan. Photo by Hans Bomskow.

Copper-Eyed White

Whites with orange or copper eyes were produced, as noted before, by mating a Blue-Eyed White to another-colored cat which had copper eyes. This was usually a Blue Persian of good type, as its purpose was to improve the type feature as well as to overcome the deafness. However, since then, they also have been bred selectively as a separate group from the Blue Eyes. The same breeding possibilities and disadvantages exist here as listed for the Blue-Eyed Whites, with the exception of those relating to eye color; naturally, those would be disadvantages that would not apply. The eye color of a Copper-Eyed White kitten should be good by the time it is eight months old. It is not likely to improve after it has passed that age.

Copper-Eyed White male owned and bred by Mrs. Harry C. Garrison: DBL. CH. GAR-LE'S GLACIER. Sire: Windibank Trinket of Gar-Le; dam: Ch. Windibank Praline.

Copper-Eyed White female owned by Mrs. D. R. Blayney: DBL. CH. PENTA-GON SNOW QUEEN OF SCIOTO. Sire: Ni-Dral Sun-Ray of Pentagon; dam: Rosedere Selena II of Ni-Dral. Bred by Mrs. Harold L. Bayer.

Copper-Eyed White male owned by Betty Lee and Rollen Junium: R.M. GR. and DBL. CH. KLINKHAMMER'S GLAMOUR BOY OF SILVER KEY. Sire: R.M. Gr. Ch. Klinkhammer's Charmer; dam: Ch. Klinkhammer's Karon. Bred by Mrs. Chris Klinkhammer.

These also are very beautiful cats. Their deep copper eyes with their snow-white coats are striking. Some of them resemble large marshmallows with raisins for eyes.

Copper-Eyed Whites have been top show winners many times in recent years, and there is much interest in breeding them to perfection. One, Gr. Ch. Shawnee Moonflight, was 1960 and 1961 Cat of the Year. His litter sister, Gr. Ch. Shawnee Soapsuds, also a Copper-Eyed White, was 1960 Opposite Sex Cat of the Year. Another well-known winner, Copper-Eyed White female Gr. Ch. Windibank Patti-Kake of Azulita, won honors as 1961 Opposite Sex Cat of the year. Her son, R.M. Gr. Ch. Azulita Pale Face of Casa Cielo, also a top show specimen, is 1963 Cat of the Year.

The Copper-Eyed Whites also seem to have the advantage of maturing early. All the cats named above, as well as many others of this color, have made spectacular show wins before reaching two years of age.

Copper-Eyed White female owned and bred by Mrs. K. C. Hopey: R.M. QUAD. CH. BLUE DIAMOND'S TAMARA. Sire: Blue Diamond's Wee Treasure; dam: Blue Diamond's White Angel.

Copper-Eyed White male owned and bred by Nikki Horner: R.M. QUAD.
GR. CHAMPION SHAWNEE MOONFLIGHT, CAT OF THE YEAR
1960 and 1961. Sire: Gr. Ch. Klinkhammer's Topper of Castalia; dam: Gr. Ch.
Shawnee Moonflower. Photo by Muzzie.

Copper-Eyed White male owned and bred by Mrs. Walker Johnston: GR.
CH. AZULITA PALEFACE OF CASA CIELO. Sire: Dixi-Land Queed of
Azulita; dam: Windibank Patti-Kake of Azulita.

XVII

BLACK PERSIANS

The Black Persian has many devoted admirers, and rightfully so. He ranks as emperor in the hierarchy of feline royalty. He is indeed a creature of beauty with his velvet-like coat and deep copper eyes like round topaz jewels. Even though his cobby body is massive with a very large head, he is always very refined looking. Most Blacks have rather aloof and reserved natures. However, they make wonderful pets and show cats, as they have a very placid and gentle disposition. A Black Persian will seldom attempt to bite or scratch while he is being groomed. The judges

Black Persian male owned by Barney and Shirley Fishel: R.M. GR. CH. TOIREH VICTORIA LE NOIR. Sire: Gr. Ch. Toireh Precious Le Noir; dam: Ch. Toireh Octavia. Bred by Celia Herriot. Photo by Gordon Laughner.

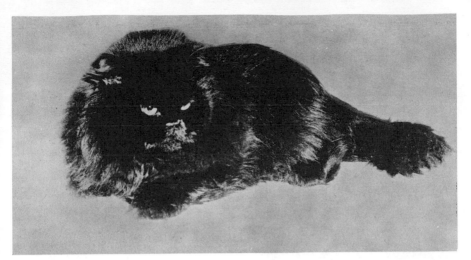

Black male owned by Richard Gebhardt and Mr. and Mrs. Robert Green: GR. CH. VELVENE VOO-DOO, CAT OF THE YEAR 1959. Sire: Gr. Ch. Lavender Liberty Beau; dam: Ch. Longhill's Black Velvet. Bred by Mr. and Mrs. Robert Green.

find them easy to handle. They sometimes are nervous at a show or with strangers, but if they should make an effort to escape, they do so in fright, not anger.

Sound Black Coloring Difficult to Maintain

It is relatively easy to get good type heads and bodies in Black breeding; however, the soundness of coat color is a problem, as it is in all the solid colors. The Black has an added problem of the coat tending to become brown or rusty in places. Also, in the cross breeding with the Blues commonly done to improve

Black female owned and bred by Mrs. Roland A. Smith: DBL. CH. WILLO-WIND BLACK MAGIC. Sire: Gr. Ch. Vel-Vene's Voo Doo; dam: Francine's Frostie of Willowind. Photo by Hollywood Photographers, Inc.

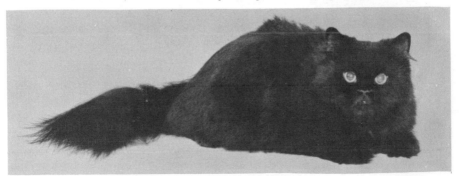

type, there is danger of the coat's graying toward the skin, instead of being the required coal black to the roots.

Helpful advice on how to try for the Best-in-Show type Black is given by Mrs. Matil Rotter, well-known CFA judge and breeder of Blacks for many years:

"To me, the pedigree is most important, and there is no other Black bloodline that stands out as does the famous Barbe Bleue strain. Gr. Ch. Pied Piper of Barbe Bleue, 1951 Cat of the Year, was the finest Black Persian I have ever had the pleasure of judging. He had a darling snub nose, tiny ears and a magnificent head."

Pied Piper has many outstanding Black progeny which carry and pass on his good features. Gr. Ch. Vel-Vene Voodoo, 1959 Cat of the Year, is descended from him and other fine cats. Voodoo, in turn, has been an excellent sire. Mrs. Rotter continues:

"Start with the finest female you can find. It is not easy to find a good Black female, as the demand is greater than the supply, and when you get one, her daily care is most important. Keep her out of the sun, which bleaches and sun-streaks the black color. If her ruff is long, put a paper

Black female owned by Mr. and Mrs. Claude Hoffman: CH. KITTEN KATS BLACK ALIBI OF DEE. Sire: Tr. Ch. Ariel's White Powder Puff; dam: Hermscrest Bonita. Bred by Edith Schulte. Photo by Gordon Laughner.

Black male owned and bred by Mrs. Claude Hoffman: CH. DEE'S SAMPSON. Sire: Gr. Ch. Pied Piper of Barbe Bleue; dam: Heart's Desire of Dee's. Photo by Wippert.

collar around her neck so she doesn't get it wet when she eats. Rusty color of Blacks and dampness of any kind go hand in hand. *Avoid dampness* whenever possible. Above all, keep her forever free of fleas! Groom her daily so that you keep out any light undercoat. Please don't think your Black Persian doesn't need a bath just because she is black. Bathing is most important, especially just before a show, or give her a thorough going over (to the skin) with a liquid evaporating-type cleaner. It will give her coat a soft clean feel that the judge will recognize and appreciate.

"A well-balanced diet is also very important to keep your Black in top condition. I feed mostly raw beef (I use a lot of beef kidney), a small amount of meal, and I add either bone meal or powdered milk for calcium. Most of my cats like the yeast tablets and eat them for treats like candy, but for the benefit of the few who don't, I add powdered yeast to the food formula. Use a little salt, too; they eat better if the food is salted a little. I feed twice a day; cats stay heavier easier by twice-daily feeding. I like to eat

149

oftener than once a day and my cats do, too. I also give a complete vitamin supplement.

"When the time comes for breeding your female, pick the best stud available. Always work to improve your stock by keeping it in top condition and breeding in extra-good bloodlines."

Mrs. Claude Hoffman, also an experienced breeder of Black Persians, adds her appreciation of the Barbe Bleue stock from which her cats are descended, and gives further suggestions on feeding and grooming:

"I have found that a teaspoon of flax-seed meal added to a diet of raw meat, wheat germ oil, and tomato juice, plus brewers yeast and kidney, makes the Blacks' coats glossy and their skin free of dry flakes. An excellent grooming trick for Blacks is the use of a black velvet mitten. Smoothed over the fur, it will remove from the coat all traces of lint or dust from the air and add that extra touch of gloss."

Black female owned by Adelaide and Toni Molino: TR. CH. SILVER MESA VELVET OF SHADO VALI. Sire: Kitten Kats Buddy Boy; dam: Silver Mesa Miss Barbara Kim. Bred by Mrs. Harold Webb. Blue female at right.

Black male owned by Mrs. J. M. Dingworth: DBL. CH. BRIARGATE'S DAVY CROCKETT OF MERU. Sire: Briargate's Symphony; dam: Ch. Kiva's Inca of Briargate.

To work up a sheen, dampen a cloth in a solution of two tablespoons of household ammonia to one quart of water, and rub it into the body fur thoroughly, working from back to front. Do this a few days before show time. Then, at the last minute, touch up lightly on tips of fur, using a cotton pad that has been dipped in this solution and squeezed out. This luster, or gloss, may be enhanced by grooming with your hands or with a piece of silk.

In breeding Blacks, the mating of color-bred Black to color-bred Black will eventually result in loss of type. If continued, the cats will tend to become big and rangy. The sound Black color is set this way, however. Most breeders favor the introduction of a dark Blue who has good type. Keep the female resulting from this type of breeding (such as a dark Blue female to a color-bred Black stud). Black bred to a good-type White has been successful, in some cases, and it does not seem to produce the problem of gray or smoky undercoat such as the cross with the Blues might.

Rusty Color of Black Kittens

Most Black kittens are very disappointing in color, and a good many have a rusty or chocolate brown appearance until seven or eight months old. Often there are white hairs sprinkled throughout the coat. These should not be present in the adult coat and usually disappear. White spots, or lockets, which are most undesirable, have been a problem, but seldom have appeared in the more recent past. A long, flowing coat is desirable, but the shorter, plushy type usually has a more even color. It has been noticed that certain strains of Black Persians do not have quite as strong a tendency to be rusty as kittens (nor do they seem to be as affected by the external causes that produce rustiness) as do other Blacks. This would be a valuable quality to try to strengthen. It may have to do with some factor of metabolism.

Black females are particularly devoted mothers, constantly washing and fondling the babies, and it has been suspected that some of the off-color in their kittens is due to the action of her saliva on their coats.

Deep Orange Eye Color Preferred

Good deep orange eye color is necessary to properly contrast with the Black coat. Years ago in England there were Blacks who had green eyes, but this eye color was eliminated in favor of the copper. Occasionally, one is seen with a faint rim of green to the orange. This is a fault, as is a pale gold eye color.

XVIII

BLUE PERSIANS

The Blue color of Persian, which is a dilute form of black, always has had wide popularity in the cat fancy. The Blue of today however, is quite different from the Blues shown at the turn of the century, and even those of a decade ago.

Blue female owned by V. V. Schuh: GR. CH. NIGRETTE PANSY OF SKY-WAY. Sire: Gr. Ch. Dixiland Montpellier Victor; dam: Gaymoor Giselle of Pom-Purr. Bred by Mrs. Walter Limpert.

Early Blues

In the early stages of their development, they were merely included in a class called Blue Tabbies (at that time meaning with tabby markings) and Blue (with or without white areas). The first all-Blue class of Persians shown at the Crystal Palace, London, in 1889, had just a few that qualified by being without any white hairs. The standard was not specific for eye color of Blue (nor of many other colors) and the head type was not stressed. Breeding for type came after the colors were clarified.

In the ten-year period following this first all-Blue class, there was great interest and activity in the breeding of Blues. They were represented by one hundred cats and kittens at the 1899 London show. Frances Simpson, of England, was one of the first

Blue female owned by Jack and Althea Wedel: TR. GR. CH. LEILANI'S LILIUOKALANI OF FIDDLER'S GREEN. Sire: Tr. Ch. Onyx Sunlight of Cresthaven; dam: Dbl. Ch. Bluelace Rosepointe of Leilani. Bred by Mrs. Fred Wildenhus.

Blue male owned by Matil Rotter: DBL. CH. BARBE BLEUE TOPS OF BRIARGATE.

to introduce this lovely cat, which gained instant popularity. The popularity and quality of Blues has increased steadily, and no doubt will continue to do so. In the United States in recent years, only the Silvers have become more plentiful than Blues. A good Blue is *always* to be reckoned with for Best-in-Show. They have had and held their top place in the shows consistently, both here and abroad, for many years.

All through the suggested breeding procedures for each Persian color, the Blue is mentioned as the best possibility to improve type. However, the breeders of Blue Persians have their problems, too. The eye color tends to fade with age. The paler shades of coat color are often accompanied by a correspondingly pale eye color. Color breeding was the usual early practice to set

155

color, and this type of breeding seems to have a tendency to cause any inherent faults to be set also. These faults appear as reversions to some feature of the type of the original Angora cat. In the Blues, it was the greater length and placement of the ears that seemed to be the most common throw-back. The early Blues were foxy-faced, had high or pricked ears, narrow muzzles and tops of heads. The narrowness of the skull accentuated the size and position of the ears. This tendency has been overcome by selective breeding, as there were many families of good Blues with which to outcross.

Blue female owned by Matil Rotter: DBL. CH. BRIARGATE'S LADY VERONICA BEAR.

Blue male owned by Mrs. A. D. Fergus: **CH. BLUE DIAMOND'S WEE LION OF FERGUS.** Sire: Blue Diamond's Wee Treasure; dam: Silver Dawn Rita Angelette of Blue Diamond. Bred by Mrs. K. C. Hopey. Photo by Maxine Reinard Studio.

Blue Type of Today Closest to Ideal

Therefore, very different are today's Blues. Now the head is very broad in a top show specimen. There is great width between the ears (which should be quite small and closed at the base). When properly groomed and carrying a full coat, the ears should be barely discernible. Eyes are large and round, expressive, and as dark a copper color as possible. The blazing reddish-copper eyes set wide apart do much to enhance this cat's beauty. Nose is extremely short and snub; cheeks are full, and the muzzle is broad and powerful. The end of the nose is a somewhat darker shade of blue than the coat, as are the lips and the whiskers, whereas the rims of the eyes are of the same color   perhaps a

157

shade darker. The paw pads have the same deeper tone, with great tufts, so that, when properly groomed, the cat may appear to be wearing huge fur slippers.

Variations in Blue Color Tone and Coat Quality

The Blue Persian of highest quality has a lavender-blue color that is the same tone over all the body. Although the trend has been toward the lighter shades of blue being more desirable, the exact shade is of less importance than its evenness of tone and the soundness of color from tip to root of each hair. The medium shades sometimes prove to be the best for these qualities. The paler the coat, the more likelihood that, upon parting the hair, it will be several shades lighter toward the skin, which is a fault. A too-dark shade of blue lacks the brightness that makes the lighter shades more attractive.

The Blue in full bloom carries a tremendous coat which, if properly groomed, accentuates the square body of this gorgeous

Blue male owned and bred by Mrs. Louise Heron: CH. HERONDALE HIS HONOUR. Sire: Gr. Ch. Woodchurch Periwinkle (Imp.); dam: Herondale Milady.

Blue female owned and bred by Mrs. Wanda Scott: QD. GR. CH. BLU ACRE FANCEE. Sire: Dbl. Ch. Silver Moth Macbeth of Blue Acre: dam: Kansas City Substitute.

cat. There are several varieties of coat: the bushy type which is a delight to groom; the long, flowing style that makes this cat with his short legs appear to be walking on his belly; and the perishable, or curly, type which is very hard to cope with. Those who have had experience with the curly type say:

"You can groom and groom up to the minute his number is called. By the time the judge gets him out on the table, his tummy looks as though he had just had an overdone permanent and a comb hadn't touched him for weeks. Then you overhear the judge remark, 'Beautiful cat; could use some grooming.' If you did not have the courage of your convictions, after spending days trying every grooming aid possible, it would be very easy to give up. However, there are many judges who recognize the curliness characteristic of this coat and allow for it."

Today's Blue Breeders Can Continue from Sound Foundation

One of our present-day well-known Blues, Gr. Ch. Dixi-land Queed of Azulita, has such a coat. His owner, Mrs. Walker T. Johnston, gives us the benefit of her years of experience in breeding, showing, and judging in the following:

"Our present-day Whites owe their splendid type to the Blue cross. For this improvement we can thank Mrs. John H. Revington, who pioneered in this achievement, going back many years to her most famous White Historian and his equally famous son, White Historian II, 1949 Opposite Sex Cat of the Year. She also imported several Blues and, in conjunction with Miss Elsie Hydon, laid a fine foundation for future Blue breeders with her Gr. Ch. Dixi-land Salute and Gr. Ch. Dixiland Pearl Harbor Yank, 1948 Cat of the Year.

Blue male owned and bred by Elsie Hydon: GR. CH. LAVENDER LIBERTY. Sire: Ch. Lavender Chu Chu; dam: Langston Delphine.

Blue male owned by Elsie Hydon: CH. LAVENDER CHU CHU (Imp.).

"Miss Hydon made trips to England every two or three years, carefully choosing and bringing back many fine cats for her own use and for other breeders. One of the most famous Blue bloodlines in the United States was started by her importation of Ch. Lavender Chu Chu. His son, Lavender Liberty, was a Grand Champion, and Liberty's son, Gr. Ch. Lavender Liberty Beau, was 1950 Cat of the Year. Chu Chu appears in practically every pedigree of a top Blue and also in top cats of other colors. To these two ladies today's breeders of Blues and Whites owe a great debt which can only be repaid by continuing to progress and carry on their work.

"The Blues are used extensively in crossing with other colors. Recently we have recognized the Blue Tabby and Blue Smoke for championship status. These cats owe much to their Blue breeding. They are truly beautiful and I am confident they will also gain in popularity, as did the Blues.

"We also have now in the fancy some very prepotent stud cats, and these are invaluable. I consider myself fortunate to own a male of this type. In every litter he sires there is at least one kitten, and sometimes two, that are exact replicas of Queed himself, and the others are all better than average. I do not mean that he is perfect—the 'perfect cat' is the one we dream about—but his very apparent good qualities are valuable to be able to reproduce. With my own Blues I prefer to line-breed and also upon occasion have mated brother and sister with excellent results. Then, from this mating, go to an out-cross, and then back to one of the grandparents.

"Many Blue kittens at birth are distinctly tabby marked. Some marks will be almost black; this could go back to the fact that blue is a dilute of black. However, by the time they are four weeks old, these markings begin to fade. Usually it is possible to tell the true color of the Blue as an adult by the color of the ears and feet of the kitten at birth.

"The disposition of the Blue is most loving and affection-

Blue male owned and bred by Mrs. Antoinette F. Wormstead: PINEWOOD BLUE SKYE. Sire: Ch. Pinewood Cher Ami; dam: Pinewood Pandora.

Blue female owned by Mrs. Paula Stephan; GR. CH. CAMBER BETSYBOB
OF ROCKY MOUNTAIN (Imp.). Bred by Mrs. Peggy Denton. Photo by
H. A. Pierson.

ate. At times you will find a male with an even sweeter
temperament than the females. Some are show-offs and
hams at heart and these are a delight for judges to handle.

Tips on Grooming of Blues

"Nothing is more beautiful than a Blue presented for
show in perfect condition. This entails a great deal of effort
and constant work on the part of his owner. Daily grooming
with particular attention to the removal of dead hair from
the coat is necessary. These hairs will be brownish or

Blue female owned by Mr. and Mrs. John Elliott: TR. CH. GALLAHAD'S JACKIE OF C-J. Sire: Evergreen's White Pine of Akanta; dam: Silver Moth's Delight of Gallahad. Bred by Blanche W. Smith.

extremely dark. The blue coat color, like the black, is also subject to rustiness from moisture and licking, and to discoloration from too much sun. It is advisable, if possible, to keep the guard hair stripped out as they appear, as they are darker. If this is not done, some cats will appear to have a black saddle when in full coat. Not all will have to be watched this closely. Some have very few guard hairs.

"During the summer months, it is often a good idea to clip the coat short. This has two advantages. The cat will be more comfortable, with less chance of hairballs forming, and the new coat will come in more evenly colored by starting afresh. However, do not let up on at least going through the pretense of grooming, lest when you do begin to prepare him for show he will be most resistant to the idea, having gotten out of the habit."

XIX

RED PERSIANS

A deep mahogany-colored Red Persian having good type and no markings or variation of color tone is seldom seen on the show bench. The standard requires this quality of color soundness for all the solid color group, but it is the most difficult to obtain in the Red Persian. Rings on the tail tip are very hard to eliminate.

Red female owned and bred by Mr. and Mrs. B. G. Ehrhardt: GR. CH. BEN-MAR SPARKLE. Sire: Kohinoor Tim O'Cream; dam: Moonfleet Tama of Ben-Mar.

The breeding of a Red Tabby to a Tortoiseshell female probably first produced a solid Red; however, it set the tendency toward markings.

A solid Red or very slightly marked Red kitten also will appear in Tabby litters, but these usually will develop more pronounced markings as they mature.

Red female owned by Jean Rose: CH. LONGHILL'S PEKE-A-BOO. Sire: Ch. Longhill's Lightning of Rosegate; dam: Eiderdown Speckle of Longhill. Bred by Anthony De Santis.

Peke-Faced cats appear spontaneously in Red Litters (see Red Tabby and Peke-Faced sections). The Peke-Faced Red is less common than the Peke-Faced Red Tabby.

In breeding for solid Reds, improvements for type and color have to be pursued independently. Introducing Blues or Blacks tends to bring out ticking and bars on the legs, although it will definitely improve type. Kittens from these breedings will be Red, Black, Tortie or Blue-Cream. The resulting Torties and Blue-Creams may be bred back to the Red sire or grandsire.

The truly solid red color can be achieved only by color breeding for many generations. Eye color is usually no problem. Excellent type and color, plus a long flowing coat and an unusual double frill around her neck, is evidenced by Ch. Shawnee Copper Lustre, Red Persian female. Her breeder, Mrs. Nikki Horner, who specialized in Tortoiseshells and Reds, considered her to be an exceptionally fine example of Red Persian.

Red males usually are quite large. The red color seems to appeal more strongly to men and to persons who themselves have the same ruddy coloring than do some of the other Persian shades.

XX

CREAM PERSIANS

Just what shade of color is meant by "cream" may be questioned, but there can be no doubt concerning the striking beauty of their big deep-amber eyes, sometimes almost brown, in their faces of pale fur.

The color of a Cream should be an even, overall shade, with

Cream male owned and bred by Mr. and Mrs. G. C. Woolman: GR. CH. WOOLMAN LA CHEDDAR. Sire: Gr. Ch. Ro-Va Phoebus of Woolman; dam: Ch. Red-Top Sue-Sue of Woolman. Photo by Abrams Photo Service.

each hair sound (i.e., same color) to its root. The most desirable shade is one that has brightness without having too much of a reddish (or "hot") cast. Too light a shade of tan or beige is likely to be insipid and dull.

Creams probably originated from lightly marked Cream Tabbies which appeared in litters of Tortoiseshells from Red Tabby sires. The Tortoiseshell has Cream splotches as well as black and red ones. These slight Tabby markings were diminished by selective breeding but still remain as a tendency.

Cream male owned and bred by Irene Powell: **QUAD. CH. CHATAMI CREME BUNNE.** Sire: Quad Ch. Chatam Autumn; dam: Dbl. Ch. Venus Mellessee.

A cross with the Blues was made, resulting in Blue-Creams. The Cream males that result from a cross between a pale Blue male and a Cream female generally are of good color and type. The opposite breeding produces good Creams of either sex.

Color breeding of Cream to Cream, after type improvements have been effected by the Blue-Cream method, is considered the most desirable procedure. Outcross, if necessary for some particular quality, to a Blue. Eye color seldom is a problem in breeding Creams.

Gr. Ch. Longhill's Michael, son of Gr. Ch. Longhill's Red Treasure, was an outstanding Cream stud. He sired outstanding Blue Cream and Cream cats, whose progeny, in turn, have carried on

Cream female owned and bred by Mr. and Mrs. B. G. Ehrhardt: GR. CH. BEN-MAR MINUET. Sire: Gr. Ch. Nor-Mont Simone's Randy; dam: Ch. Willowood Sapphire of Ben-Mar. Photo by Joseph Spies.

Cream female owned and bred by Mr. and Mrs. G. C. Woolman: GR. CH. WOOLMAN TICKLED PINK. Sire: Gr. Ch. Ro-Va Phoebus of Woolman; dam: Gr. Ch. Woolman. Photo by Abrams Photo Service.

Cream male owned and bred by Mrs. John Bloem: **GR. CH. BLOEMHILL SPARTAN.** Sire: Nigrette's Tereus of Bloemhill; dam: Ch. Bloemhill Lorelei. Photo by Smitty's.

Cream male owned by Mrs. Merald Hoag: **GR. CH. CHEZ MOUMETTE CAL OF NOR-MONT, CAT OF THE YEAR, 1962.** Sire: Ch. Longhill's Super Mike; dam: Longhill's Michelina. Bred by Peggy Owen.

Cream male owned and bred by Mr. and Mrs. B. G. Ehrhardt: CH. BEN-MAR DAYDREAM. Sire: Gr. Ch. Nor-Mont Simone's Randy; dam: Ch. Willowood Cameo of Ben Mar. Photo by Sentinel Star Pictures.

his qualities through several different-color families. Gr. Ch. Chez Moumette Cal of Normont, 1962 Cat of the Year, is his grandson.

Mrs. John Bloem, who has bred many lovely Creams and Blue-Creams, offers this advice on evaluating Cream kittens:

"Do not keep for breeding or showing any kitten having even the faintest leg bar or Tabby marking. This marking will become evident when the kitten is but a few days old and will never disappear. True, they become less noticeable when the coat is full, but they are still present, and are a fault. The true Cream color does not arrive until the cat's second winter as an adult. The first winter they are apt to show a reddish tinge, but that fades as the cat ages. Also, ears that are too long in a kitten will remain so in its adulthood."

Most of the good Cream cats of today have a great deal of Blue

Cream male owned by Mrs. Samy Hirsig: QUAD. CH. CHADHURST
SUNSHINE OF ROCKY MOUNTAIN (Imp.). Bred by Miss L. Rodda,
England. Photo by H. A. Pierson.

Cream female owned by Mrs. Richard Maier: R.M. GR. CH. and CH. MIN-
QUA'S SUNBEAM OF STARMIST. Sire: Minqua's Shamus; dam: Minqua's Roberta. Bred by Mr. and Mrs. Thomas L. Martinke.

**Cream male owned by Mrs. Jean Rose: GR. CH. LONGHILL'S MICHAEL.
Sire: Gr. Ch. Longhill's Red Treasure; dam: Eiderdown Phian of Seacrest.
Bred by Anthony DeSantis.**

in their background, and have inherited equal type. Care must
be exercised in the breeding of Creams, as well as all of the other
solid colors from Blues, so that they do not go over the line
into Peke Faces, for which there is no class except in Red and
Red Tabby colors. If the nose becomes too short and flat, breathing difficulties will ensue, and the tear duct passage may be
unable to drain the eyes, resulting in dripping, running eyes that
stain the surrounding fur.

Creams are usually sweet-tempered and gentle, perhaps a little
shy.

XXI

BLUE CREAM PERSIANS

The Standard for Blue Creams calls for a combination of the paler shades of the two colors, with Blue predominating. They and the Torties, who are patched similarly but in different colors, may be called the "pansy faces" in the cat garden due to the striking beauty of their irregular face markings.

The Blue Creams inherit their good type and eye color from Blue and Cream parentage, their perfection depending on soundness of color, with the added problem of its distribution to best advantage without any mixing of the two.

Blue Cream female owned and bred by Mrs. John Bloem; GR. CH. BLOEM-HILL MISS IOWA. Sire: Gr. Ch. Bloemhill Spartan; dam: Ch. Longhill's Misty Moon. Photo by Abrams Photo Service.

Again, we are indebted to Mrs. Bloem for her description of this color patching:

"It is preferable to have Blue Cream kittens born with less cream visible than would be desired in the adult coat, as the cream markings have a tendency to become more pronounced as the kitten matures, and blue must always be the dominant color. A well-marked face is essential and should be divided in color, but with more blue than cream. A ruff that is partly cream, with the cream extending up and into the chin, is a beautiful feature. The body, too, should have cream patches. In grooming, these should be highlighted by combing in such a manner that they show plainly. The feet should be splashed with color; all four feet is ideal, but not necessary."

Blue Cream female owned by Dr. and Mrs. F. M. Williams: GR. CH. LADY BESS OF PENSFORD. Sire: Foxburrow Frivolous; dam: Dawn of Pensford. Bred by Miss Joan Thompson. Photo by *Courier-Journal* and *Louisville Times.*

Blue Cream female owned and bred by Mrs. John Bloem: CH. BLOEMHILL LORELEI. Sire: Ch. Bloemhill's Aladin; dam: Bloemhill Lilliput.

Strangely enough, the patching that is called for in the American Standard is undesirable in England, where they prefer the colors intermingled without division, producing the effect of shot silk.

Blue Cream is a sex-linked color; kittens are almost always females. If any Blue Cream males are born, they usually die at an early age.

There are four "recipes" for producing Blue Creams. These combinations and their predictable results are as follows: (You would have similar color results by using Red instead of Cream, but this is not recommended breeding for best Blue Creams, as it would tend to make "hot" patches.)

When a Blue male is mated to either a Blue Cream or Cream female, the kittens can be Blue Cream females, Blue females, Blue males or Cream males. Cream females never result from this breeding.

A Cream male bred to a Blue Cream female will produce Blue Cream females, Cream females, Blue males, or Cream males. No

Blue Cream female owned and bred by Mrs. Jack Wedel: FIDDLER'S GREEN APRIL RAIN. Sire: Burque-Lee Honey B'ar of Fiddler's Green; dam: Dbl. Ch. Fiddler's Green Adventuress.

Blue females come from this breeding.

No Blue kittens of either sex will result when a Cream male is bred to a Blue female. This breeding produces only Cream males and Blue Cream females.

The best marked Blue Creams seem to result when the stud is a Cream.

Since this breeding is primarily to improve the Creams or to produce high-quality Blue Creams, the Blues of such matings customarily are not used for Blue breeding.

The points for color in the judging scale are divided between the color and the markings of Blue Creams.

XXII

SILVER PERSIANS

The effect of a Silver Persian's coloring could be described as white, but when a Silver is placed next to a White Persian there is a marked difference. Under a microscope, a strand of hair appears tubular. Whereas a White's hair is solidly filled with white pigment, the Silver's hair shaft is nearly empty. The silver-colored effect results from light reflecting off each translucent hair.

There are two color varieties of Silver Persian: the lighter is called Chinchilla Silver; the darker, Shaded Silver. They both are referred to as Silvers, as they have the same origins and general characteristics. You may get both varieties in a litter of kittens.

Chinchilla male owned and bred by Mr. and Mrs. Harold Webb: GR. CH. SILVER MESA SIR VALLIANT. Sire: Ch. Sir Pixie of Silver Mesa; dam: Cecelia Scotia of Silver Mesa. Photo by Gordon Laughner.

Chinchilla Silver male owned by Mrs. Harry C. Garrison: DBL. GR. and TR. CH. LAS MONTANAS SILVER THISTLE. Sire: Las Montanas Flying Cloud; dam: Kini's Rag Doll de Las Montanas. Bred by Mel Russell. Photo by Ab - rams Photo Service.

Chinchilla female owned and bred by Mrs. Ivan Over: DBL. CH. GRAY IVY TOY ANN and trophy won for Miss Cat World 1959. Sire: Quad Ch. Gray Ivy Aladdin; dam: Wee Heather Holly Ann of Gray Ivy. Photo by Gordon Laughner.

Chinchilla male owned by J. Van Zele: TR. GRAND. CH. KERRY LU
RAMON OF CASA CONTENTA. Sire: Beverly-Serrano Jody of Kerry Lu;
Dam: Ben Fair Twilight Melody. Bred by Lucy and Carrie Clingan.

Chinchilla male owned and bred by Gladys Weirich: GR. CH. SKYLAND
ARCTURUS. Sire: Dbl. Ch. Hi-Ho Silver; dam: Tr. Ch. Skyland Diana.
Photo by Hodgdon Studios.

Silver Persians are thought by many to be the most spectacular
of all longhaired cats. They are the most popular color variety
in the United States.

Mascara Markings

The first thing you notice about a Silver is his eyes. They are
characterized particularly by a rim of dark pigment on the edge
of the eyelids. A heavy smudge, or streak of black tipping,
immediately below the eyes gives the impression that the cat is
wearing eye makeup and that the mascara has smudged. The
eye color itself is outstandingly beautiful. It ranges from emerald
green to turquoise blue of intense shades. The deeper the color
the better, for a good show specimen. The eyes are extremely
large and round, and set wide apart. Silvers and Silver Tabbies
are the only Persians who have green or blue-green eyes..

Chinchilla male owned and bred by V. O. Peterson: DBL. GR. and QUINT. CH. BEVERLY-SERRANO KEO. Sire: Babe Le Roy of Beverly-Serrano; dam: Beverly-Serrano Honey. Photo by Gordon Laughner.

The nose and mouth are also edged in black. The white whiskers often are dark-shafted just where they start from the muzzle. These facial markings enable one to see every play of expression. In fact, the whole face looks as if it were embroidered with black silk on silvery white velvet.

Other Characteristics of Silvers

The brick-red center of the nose is a characteristic Silver beauty mark. It should be a deep brick-red color to contrast with the very light-colored muzzle and chin fur; it should be black-edged.

The Silver coat is of a much lighter and finer texture than most of the other colors. The hair grows in "angel tufts," or "horns," springing from the tophead. These start up alongside the ears, to stand up, sometimes above the ears themselves. Many Silvers also have long feathery hairs that curl out and around the head, starting from the inside front edge of the ears. The whole coat, being light in weight and finely textured, can be combed and groomed to stand away from the body in a cloud effect, giving an ethereal look.

To live up to their full potential of beauty, the Silvers must have—to a marked degree—the extremely sweet "baby face" expression that is desirable in all colors. The smiling mouth, the made-up face of a coquette, and all the frills of their fancy coat have earned them the title "The Cadillac of Cats."

Chinchilla female R.M. GR. and QUINT. CH. DEARHEART TINA MARIE. Sire: Ch. Dearheart Mario; dam: Reene's Marie of Dearheart. Photo by Hans Bomskow.

Chinchilla female owned by V. O. Peterson: DBL. GR. CH. CHIQUITA
LINDA OF BEVERLY-SERRANO. Sire: Leo of Allington; dam: Wahoo
Lady Cozette. Bred by Jessie Hazlett. Photo by Gordon Laughner.

Chinchilla male owned and bred by Dr. and Mrs. P. N. Ramsdale: CH. DEARHEART MARIO. Sire: Dearheart Sir Winston; dam: Beauty of Dream Harbor. Photo by Louise Van der Meid.

Chinchilla Silvers

The ideal coat color of a Chinchilla Silver is light silver-white. There should be sufficient black tipping evenly sprinkled over the cheeks, head, back, flanks, outside of legs, and topside of tail to give a frosted look. Tipping should shade off gradually to a clear white on the ruff, muzzle, chin, chest, belly, inside of legs, and underside of tail. Even at first glance, there should be no confusion as to whether a cat is a Chinchilla Silver or a White Persian with green eye color.

Shaded Silvers

The proper Shaded Silver coloring gives an entirely different appearance from that of a Chinchilla. Where the general effect

Chinchilla Silver female owned by Edith and Aaron Vaughan: CH. PRIN-CESS BELITA (SPAY). Sire: Beverly-Serrano Jody of Kerry Lu; dam: Ben Fair Twilight Melody. Photo by Gordon Laughner.

Chinchilla Silver female owned and bred by Irene Powell: CH. CHATAMI FLAIRE. Sire: Ch. Capistrano Son of Lit'l Kat; dam: Silver Dawn Lauralee.

Chinchilla male owned by Helen Amos: DBL. GR. CH. MICHAEL OF BEVERLY-SERRANO. Sire: Gr. Ch. Duffy of Beverly-Serrano; dam: Mitzi of Beverly-Serrano. Bred by Jessie Hazlett. Photo by Peter Gowland.

of a Chinchilla is sparkling white with coal black dusting, the Shaded has an overlay of coloring in the shaded areas that is like a lavender-gray or pewter patina, clearly defined from the lighter underparts. Shaded Silvers are best appreciated from a little distance away. The shading should give the impression that molten silver has been brushed on the coat. All shading—on the face, head, back, flanks, outside half of the legs and topside of the tail—should be of the same intensity. No streaks, blotches, or stripes should be evident in the shading, all of which should be considerably darker, in total effect, than the tipping of a Chinchilla. It should present a sharp, clearly outlined contrast where it meets with the clear white of the ruff, muzzle, chin, chest, inner half of the legs, belly, and underside of the tail.

If there is any doubt whether a particular Silver is Chinchilla

Chinchilla male owned and bred by Mrs. Donald Buchan: R.M. QUINT. CH. WEE HEATHER RAEBURN. Sire: Tr. Ch. Wee Heather Scotty; dam: Olah Laurie of Wee Heather. Photo by Don Martin.

Chinchilla Silver female owned and bred by Mrs. C. A. Coughlin: GR. and TR. CH. CO-MC'S SILVER CHERUB. Sire: Co-Mc's Silver Venture; dam: Ch. Gar-Le's -Adoree of Co-Mc.

Chinchilla female owned by Margaret Lovett: GR. and QUINT. CH. MARLEON SPRINGTIME CAPRICE. Sire: Kute Kit Silver Signature II; dam: Quad Gr. Ch. Casa Contenta Caprice. Photo by *Newark News.*

Chinchilla male owned by Leon Lovett: QUAD. CH. MARLEON KILE. Sire: Kute Kit Noel Star; dam: Quad Gr. Ch. Casa Contenta Caprice. Bred by Margaret Lovett.

Chinchilla Silver female owned by Dr. and Mrs. P. N. Ramsdale: DBL. CH. REENE'S SUSETTE OF DEARHEART. Sire: Ch. Sir Pixie of Silver Mesa; dam: Reene's Calette. Bred by Irene Laffoon. Photo by Gordon Laughner.

or Shaded in coloring, his color is not proper to either category at that time. He would be penalized for color if he were shown.

The question of which of the two types of Silver coloring is the most desirable is entirely a matter of personal preference. They are equally beautiful, although quite different. Good, even Shaded coloring is harder to get than good Chinchilla color.

If you fall in love with a particular kitten, it really doesn't matter
which color or which breed she is; the love of a cat is what truly mat-
ters and cats are intelligent enough to know when they are loved.
Photo by C.L.I.

Chinchilla female owned by Margaret Lovett. QUAD. GR. CH. CASA CONTENTA CAPRICE. Sire: Kinnikinnick de las Montanas; dam: Casa Contenta Donna Isabelle. Bred by Helen Van Zele.

Breeding of Silvers

In Persians, the Silver color has been "set" in the Chinchillas and Shadeds through many generations of color-breeding. In spite of the inherent difficulties of reversion to Angora type that are likely to be encountered by continuing to do so, I feel that this is still the best procedure. In my opinion, a Silver cat can be bred only to another Silver to maintain the green or blue-green eye color, brick-red nose, face markings, and clear coat color. As a general rule, when a Silver is mated to a Persian of another color for type improvement, any one or all of the features which make this variety distinctive are lost. By the time these qualities are recovered, any gain is questionable.

The Silver strain should be kept intact and unmixed with any other. When improvements are needed in bone or type, careful selection of a Silver mate that does have the desired qualities is the proper procedure. There is a definite challenge in the breeding of Silvers. Breeders strive to match the solid colors in heavy

Shaded Silver male owned by Dorothy Hare: **QUAD. CH. CHARMENTE OF PURR-MEW.** Sire: Gr. Ch. Don Roberto of Beverly Serrano; dam: Nina of Silver Gables. Bred by Lucile Laird.

Shaded Silver male owned by Louise Heron: **CH. HERONDALE CARLOS.** Sire: Ch. Chateau Chat Le Magnifique of Silver Key; dam: Shy Pines Cristal of Herondale.

Chinchilla female owned and bred by Dr. and Mrs. P. N. Ramsdale: DEAR-HEART FANTASIA. Sire: Tr. Ch. Sir Anthony Dearheart; dam: Fancy Lady of Dearheart. Photo by Louise Van der Meid.

Black male owned by Carolyn Topping: GR. CH. BLUE CHECK'S KING TUT OF TOPS KAT. Sire: Dbl. Ch. Trino of Blue Check; dam: Dark Desire of Goforth. Bred by Mrs. Ada Dally. Photo by Louise Van der Meid.

Red Tabby Peke-faced male owned and bred by Dr. and Mrs. F. M. Williams: GR. CH. COLONIAL KING PETER. Sire: Gr. Ch. Rustnik Johnnie; dam: Far-Fin Beatrice. Photo by Marie Williams.

Brown Tabby male owned and bred by Mr. and Mrs. James Elliott: CH. GLEN-LYN MR. CHIPS. Sire: Tr. Ch. Glen-Lyn Don Tomas; dam: Dbl. Ch. Silver Vista Peachy Miss. Photo by Louise Van der Meid.

Chinchilla female owned by V. O. Peterson. QUINT. GR. CH. LA CHATA OF BEVERLY-SERRANO. Sire: Fanfare of Allington (Imp.); dam: Charisse of Beverly-Serrano. Bred by Jessie Hazlett. Photo by Gordon Laughner.

bone and equal their body type by careful breeding. It has been done successfully by many in recent years. There is no necessity for Silvers to be frail-boned in order to have the beautiful ethereal look that is their trademark.

The Beverly-Serrano strain of Silvers has been one of the best known of the American families. The introduction, from time to time, of a Chinchilla English import has proved very successful. Their respective good qualities blend together very well, which is not always so in outcrossing. Most of the Silver cats pictured in this book are either direct from this line or have it in their background.

Silvers are slow developing as to general appearance, yet they may reach sexual maturity earlier than other Persians. At only six months of age some males have sired kittens—their own idea, of course. Their slowness in acquiring the general appearance of maturity presents a problem in evaluating kittens and young adults, especially where a breeder is yet in the process of determining the potential of his stock, as their coat coloring, type, and eye color can improve to a marked degree after the age of two, even three, years. However, this slowness is being overcome by selective breeding. A careful study of family trends in the pedigree will give an idea as to which features are most likely to develop. Although originally closely related, each of the various Silver families has developed its individual tendencies, both good and bad, which may be traced in its progeny quite easily.

Shaded Silver male owned by Mr. and Mrs. Harold Webb: GR. CH. SIR BEDFORD OF PICKFORD SQUARE. Sire: Dbl. Gr. Ch. Michael of Beverly-Serrano; dam: Aphrodisia of Pickford Square. Bred by Mrs. Wesley Boyd.

Seal Point Himalayan kitten bred by Goforth Cattery. Photo by Louise Van der Meid.

How often has a boyfriend or husband brought home a rose and a precious kitten. . . as the ultimate in showing how much he loves his "gal." If you want your man to get the idea, just leave this page open for him to read! Photo by C.L.I.

Shaded Silver spay owned by Mr. and Mrs. Ed. Stanoszyk: **PREMIER TERI JEANNE OF DEARHEART** and actress Jayne Mansfield. Sire: Gr. Ch. Beverly Serrano Roger of Dearheart; dam: Dearheart Lady Lisabette. Bred by Angie Picchi.

Shaded Silver male owned and bred by Mr. and Mrs. D. R. Blayney: DBL. CH. SCIOTO SILVER LADD. Sire: Gr. Ch. Scioto's Valparaiso; dam: Chateau Chat Nanette of Scioto.

Shaded Silver male owned by Mrs. Robert Weston. QUINT. CH. LAS LOMAS JULIO OF WALNUT HILL. Sire: Quad. Ch. Las Lomas Man About Town; dam: Silver Mesa Miss Pixie. Bred by Doris Cook.

Cats have eyes which are completely different from those of dogs. The permanent eye color of a cat may take as long as two years to "clear" or "come in," as many cat breeders say. It is not always possible to predict the eye color of an adult cat from studying the kitten's eyes unless you have some previous experience with the same genetic line. Photo by C.L.I.

Chinchilla Silver female owned by Dr. and Mrs. P. N. Ramsdale: DBL. CH. REENE'S SUSETTE OF DEARHEART. Sire: Ch. Sir Pixie of Silver Mesa; dam: Reene's Calette. Bred by Mrs. Irene Laffoon. Photo by Harry Stuart.

Himalayan Seal Point female (left) and Himalayan Blue Point male (right), both owned and bred by Mrs. Marguerita Goforth: GOFORTH'S MONIQUE and GOFORTH'S BLU MOON. Sire (for both): Ch. Goforth's Chocolate Soldier; dam (for both): Dbl. Ch. Goforth's Mona Lisa. Photo by Louise Van der Meid.

Shaded Silver female owned by Jeanne Ramsdale and Irene Laffoon: CH. REENE'S NOLA OF DEARHEART. Sire: Gr. Ch. Beverly Serrano Roger of Dearheart; dam: Delphi Nola of Reene's. Bred by Irene Laffoon. Photo by Gordon Laughner.

For example, in some Silver lines, the permanent eye color "comes in" as soon as the baby blue starts to change, which is between six and eight weeks of age. In others, it goes through many changes of color and depth until the cat is eighteen months to two years of age, at which time the then-attained color becomes permanent.

In my experience, however, the most desirable and beautiful green or blue-green eye color usually manifests itself in the adult when the kitten's eyes show purple and turquoise flecks in their very deep blue color at about four to six weeks. This type has a depth and intensity that does not change or fade no matter how old the cat becomes.

Another change that is noticed in some families is that the kittens have noses with black, or nearly black, centers. Black is not the proper nose-leather color for adult Silvers. These dark noses will usually lighten, taking varying lengths of time to do so. When they do, they become the very epitome of the color

Shaded Silver male owned by Irene Laffoon: CH. FALCON OF DEAR-HEART. Sire: Dbl. Gr. Ch. Beverly-Serrano Roger of Dearheart; dam: Antoinette of Belmont. Bred by Adele Magill. Photo by Hans Bomskow.

called for in the Standard, a clear, deep, brick-red. If the nose center remains too dark or has a muddy color in adulthood, it is an undesirable trait to be overcome in future breeding. Equally undesirable is the tendency noticed in other families for the nose leather to be pink, or pale in the center, or have little or no black edging. When a Silver is bred to another color of Persian, either one of these faults is likely to appear in the kittens of the first generation and also in their following progeny.

Silver Kittens Are Not Silver-Colored at Birth

All Silver kittens are born speckled or patterned, some to a greater degree than others. Many have complete tabby markings of black or gray on white or are quite dark on their backs and

Many kittens change colors as they mature. Silver kittens, for example, may be born speckled or patterned, but your cat breeder can tell you the ultimate color to which a particular kitten will mature. This lovely kitten will probably stay the same color. Photo by C.L.I.

Shaded Silver male owned and bred by Dr. and Mrs. P. N. Ramsdale: R.M. QUAD. CH. DEARHEART DANIEL. Sire: Ch. Dearheart Mario. Photo by Don Martin.

tails. Those with the least coloring do not necessarily turn into Chinchillas as they grow up. In some families, they do; in others, they don't. Usually, though not always, the kittens having little or no markings on their heads, faces, and legs will be the Chinchillas, and vice versa. Fur often is quite short on the newborn, so that all you see are the very tips of the top coat. As the kittens grow older, they get lighter day by day, and the pattern diffuses or spreads out as the top coat grows longer and the undercoat comes in.

Shaded Silver male owned and bred by Mrs. D. R. Blayney: R.M. GR. CH. SCIOTO'S VALPARAISO. Sire: Ch. Beau-Sing of Nine Lives; dam: Citrus Ridge Heather of Scioto.

Longhaired cats require constant grooming. Many longhaired cats require daily combing, but the real trouble usually starts in tangles and mats in the undercoat. Examine your longhair as often as possible, certainly at least once a day; as you stroke her, carefully run your fingers deeply into the undercoat and feel for knots, tangles and mats. Its much easier to solve hair problems as soon as they start. Photo by C.L.I.

It will not be easy to guess the final color of this kitten's eyes until the permanent eye color "comes in." Photo by C.L.I.

Shaded Silver male owned by Betty Lee and Rollen Junium: CHATEAU CHAT LE MAGNIFIQUE OF SILVER KEY. Sire: R.M. Gr. Ch. Rollywood Michael II; dam: Ch. Robelaine's Renown. Bred by Sally B. Kisler.

Shaded Silver male owned and bred by Ada May Miles: TR. CH. KIVA SHADDO. Sire: Kelita of Bantam Ranch; dam: Kiva Cochiti. Photo by Gordon Laughner.

Can't you picture an unaware novice breeder, who, having bred his Silver to a Silver stud, is presented with a litter of very dark, very short-haired kittens—with stripes? Gad!

The definite markings usually fairly well disappear by four to six weeks, starting at the head, the rings on the tail being the last to go. By that time, the kittens have a fluffy coat and are very attractive, as are Persian kittens of any color! Scampering about, they look so cute from the rear, with their fur chaps and Christmas-tree tails.

Grooming of Silvers

The skin of a Silver is tender and delicate. Guard against any skin irritation which might cause the coat to come out by the

Shaded Silver female owned by Barbara Essig Hodson: R.M. GR. and QUINT. CH. BONNIE MEMORY OF SHASTA. Sire: Tr. Ch. Bonnie Sterling Silver; dam: Bonnie Carolina Rose. Bred by Mrs. A. E. Townsend. Photo by Gordon Laughner.

This kitten earns more than you would imagine. She is a professional cat model; she poses for the camera as though she were human and she is so well trained that she serves well for television commercials. Since cats are so difficult to train (compared to dogs), and since there is such a great demand for television shorts to advertise cat foods, well-trained cats are highly paid. Photo by C.L.I.

Shaded Silver male owned by Dr. and Mrs. P. N. Ramsdale: QUINT. CH.
BEVERLY-SERRANO ROGER OF DEARHEART. Sire: Tr. Ch. Sir Anthony
of Dearheart; dam: Beverly-Serrano Mar-E. Bred by V. Osburn Peterson.
Photo by Louise Van der Meid.

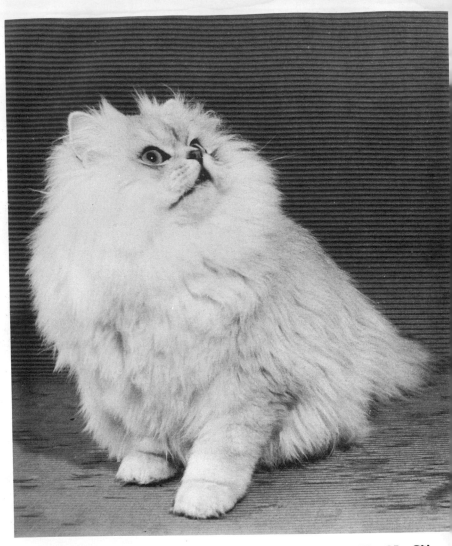

Shaded Silver male owned by Jeanne Ramsdale: R.M. DBL. GR. CH. BEVERLY-SERRANO ROGER OF DEARHEART. Sire: Tr. Ch. Sir Anthony Dearheart; dam: Beverly-Serrano Mar-E. Bred by V. O. Peterson. Photo by Gordon Laughner.

handful. Also, the undercoat tangles and mats easily, so particular care must be taken to keep it from felting. This is accomplished by daily combing.

At times, when a Chinchilla's coat is in the process of shedding, he may look darker than a Shaded Silver. Closer inspection will reveal that the dark effect is from the tips of the dead, or dying, guard hairs. These may be stripped out by hand to hasten

Shaded Silver male owned and bred by Jessie Hazlett: GR. CH. DUFFY OF BEVERLY-SERRANO. Sire: Starlight Heart Bandit II; dam: Chiquita Linda.

Shaded Silver male owned by Edna Nebergall: DBL. GR. and QT. CH. BEVERLY-SERRANO SIR PATRICK. Sire: Beverly-Serrano Keochat; dam: Beverly-Serrano Jinny. Bred by V. Osburn Peterson.

Walter Chandoha, the world's most famous cat photographer, took this photo for our cover. It is one of his favorites.

The personalities of many Persians and longhairs are as different as the breeds. Silvers have a personality all their own, as does almost every other color variety. If you are interested in a pet cat, discuss the personalities of the various colors with the cat breeder from whom you are purchasing your kitten. It is very important that you select a kitten whose personality is compatible with your own. Photo by C.L.I.

Shaded Silver female owned and bred by Ruth Essig: R.M. DBL. GR. and QUAD. CH. SHASTA NAPUA. Sire: Tr. Ch. Gray Ivy Danemora of Wee Heather; dam: Shasta Cindy. Photo by Gordon Laughner.

the procedure. When they are ready to come out, they will do so easily. The Shadeds, also, may have their dead hair stripped out to good advantage.

The Silver Personality

The Silver personality is one of the most interesting of all the varieties of Persians, differing in a way difficult to describe. They can be quite demanding, temperamental, and independent. On the other hand, many are extremely affectionate, and demonstrate it by hugging, head-butting, and holding you with their paws. Quite a few of them are very talkative. Silvers are particularly given to developing little daily routines of their own. Most persons who have known and once succumbed to the charm and beauty of a Silver cannot imagine ever not having one of their own to enjoy.

222

XXIII

BLUE SMOKE AND BLACK SMOKE PERSIANS

The Smoke in full coat is spectacularly beautiful. At first glance one sees what appears to be a Black Persian with a light silver ruff and ear tufts. However, upon parting the fur with the fingers or blowing on his coat, the white undercoat will be revealed. This white undercoat will be found all over the cat: legs and feet, body, tail, and face—even the ears. The belly is smoky in appearance, rather than black, but underneath will be found the white. True Smoke coloring will not be found any-

Blue Smoke male (neuter) owned by Mrs. Pauline Stewart: H.M. QUAD. CH. SILVER DAWN'S LI'L GUY OF DEN LEE. Sire: Blue Diamond's Wee Treasure; dam: Silver Dawn's Cinderella's Pumpkin. Bred by Mrs. Max Eckenburg.

Red Tabby Peke-faced male owned by Pauline Frankenfield: CH. ELCO'S TINY TIM OF ANGELITA. Sire: Ch. Far Fin's Don Jose; dam: Tr. Ch. Viking Cinderella of Elco. Bred by Ella Conroy. Photo by Louise Van der Meid.

Blue Cream female owned by Helen Hamlin: CH. CATILIA BELLA ADORA OF EL GATITO. Sire: Normont Beige Gentleman; dam: Silver Moth Serana of Catilia. Bred by Marcena Myers. Photo by Louise Van der Meid.

Blue Smoke female owned and bred by V. V. Schuh: GR. CH. SKYWAY'S PAULETTE. Sire: Skyway's Paul of Evergreen; dam: Skyway's Trinket.

where, but the "points," such as the face, legs, and tail, should appear as solid a black as possible, with no stripes or tabby markings.

It is fascinating to watch a Smoke jump or walk across a room and see the white undercoat rippling under the black. He gives the effect of being clothed in shot silk.

The eyes should be big, round, and of a deep copper color, looking out of a black face framed in a silver frill. The nose leather, lips, and rims of the eyes should be black. Smokes of earlier years used to have green or hazel eyes, but when they were crossed with the Blacks and Blues for type improvements the eye color requirement was changed to orange or copper, deep copper being preferred.

As the other color requirements are the same for Blue Smokes and Black Smokes, the description and breeding of Blue Smokes would be exactly the same as that for Black Smokes, substituting

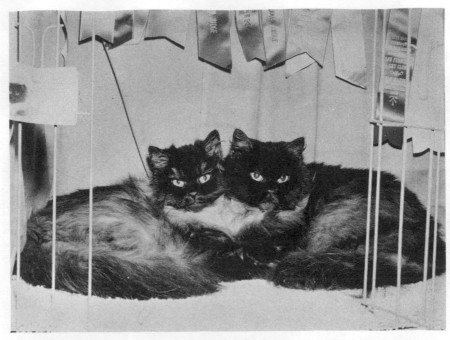

Black Smoke females owned and bred by Winifred Miles: (right) QUAD. CH. SPRING MOUNTAIN WHIMSY, (left) TR. CH. SPRING MOUNTAIN JUNO. Sire: Nuikane Rania of Spring Mountain; dam: Spring Mountain Cinderella. Photo by Gilman.

Black Smoke female, Black Smoke male, and Blue male owned by Mrs. Matil Rotter: CH. SWEETIE OF BRIARGATE. CH. IMP. BRIARGATE BENJAMIN OF GIPPESWYK; CH. BARBE BLEUE TOPS OF BRIARGATE.

Black Smoke female owned and bred by Winifred C. Miles: CH. SPRING MOUNTAIN JOYOUS. Sire: Dbl. Ch. Nui Kane Rania of Spring Mountain; dam: Ch. Spring Mountain Cinderella.

"blue" for "black" whenever mentioned. The Smoke cat has been in existence as a distinct type of color variety for many years. An early English show catalog mentions a class of twelve female Smokes in 1894.

The origin of Smoke coloring is unknown. Several different theories are advanced, the most common being that the Smokes and the Silvers had a common origin in the Silver Tabby, the Smokes being the extremely dark variety in which the genes for markings were lost, thereby producing a solid-color overlay to the silver white ground color. The Silvers, Chinchilla, and Shaded are the lightest and least marked of the family. About 1900 there was a color of Persian called Masked Silver which is not seen anymore. From their pictures, these cats seemed to resemble Silvers having black faces and legs, similar to the "points" of a

Siamese. Some geneticists think there is a link between the gene for the Siamese color pattern and the gene for silverness. No one knows which cart came before which horse, but it is safe to assume that they are all variations of the same theme, either produced by mutation or by accidental cross-breeding to a Solid Color. (The Cameo is a new variation of Silver cross-breeding, the developments of which might help unravel the intertwined origins.)

How to Tell You Have a Smoke Kitten

Mrs. Paul Raine, of Fair Oaks Cattery, gives us her opinion:
A Smoke kitten is born a Smoke kitten. They look like black

Black Smoke female owned and bred by Mrs. Gladys Weirich: CH. SKYLAND LORELEI. Sire: Dbl. Ch. Skyland Orion of Glen Lyn; dam: Ch. Skyland Candice. Photo by Hans Bomskow.

Black Smoke mother and Kittens owned by R. M. Dalrymple: GR. and QUAD. CH. SKYWAY SMOKEY ELLA and kittens. Sire: Nigrette's Hercules of Skyway; dam: Wheeler's Bunny Love. Bred by V. V. Schuh.

chiffon velvet at birth, but if you look closely you will see a smudge of whitish tipping around the eyes and on the muzzle. The stomach will be grayish, and the front legs and paws will have a definite charcoal cast. The undercoat along the spine will probably be black at this time, but sometimes upon parting the hair on the flanks the grayish white that is the start of the undercoat will be seen. The underside of the tail will also have this type of coloring. As time goes on, the Smoke kitten is a fascinating little fellow to observe. As his coat grows, his color becomes more apparent and the silvery markings become more pronounced. The white undercoat becomes noticeable at about three weeks and gradually becomes more so. By the time a kitten is six or eight weeks old, he assumes a rather mottled appearance, with the undercoat showing through the topcoat. Usually by six months of age he is quite presentable, his topcoat having returned to its original jet black and the undercoat having developed fully. He then is ready for his first show.

The kitten who develops the white undercoat next to the skin when only a few days or a week old will be the adult with the best undercoat. The copper eye color takes about a year to develop fully, but if he does not have eyes of some shade of copper by the time he is five months old, he will not have deep-copper eyes as an adult. It would be wise to pick your Smoke kitten for type when he is approximately five weeks of age.

The Problem in the Breeding of Smokes

Smokes cannot be color-bred to other Smokes for any length of time before tabby markings appear and type disappears. Smokes are usually crossed back and forth with Black from a Blue background in order to retain eye color and type. You can

Black Smoke female owned by Joan Rosemont; TR. CH. NANI-LEI U'I UHINI OF CHAT ENCORE. Sire: Quad. Ch. Nani-Lei King Lani Lei; dam: Ch. San Mateo Star of Nani-Lei. Bred by Mildred A. Joseph.

Black Smoke male owned by Conrad Rosemont: CH. CHAT ENCORE BAD BASCOMBE. Sire: Quin. Ch. Blue Check King Tut of Tops-Kats; dam: San Mateo Summer Storm. Bred by Joan Rosemont.

use a Blue, alone, but Black is preferred for Black Smokes, particularly since the Blue tends to muddy the undercoat and give a bluish cast to the black topcoat.

Some Smoke breeders feel that the introduction of a Copper-Eyed White from a background of Blue, White, and Smoke is the best way to gain everything you are striving for. If such a Copper-Eyed White is bred to a Smoke from Black and Smoke ancestry, all of the desired elements should be there. However, nature's plans do not always coincide with ours, so there can be many failures before you happen on the precise breeding which will produce good Smokes for you. It seems to be the rule that Smokes will appear only if both parents have Smoke somewhere in their backgrounds.

Black is one of the dominant colors, and in a Black-and-Smoke breeding the majority of the kittens probably will be Black. Even in the mating of two Smokes, if there is a Black in their pedigrees, one or two of the kittens will be Black. These Blacks may appear to be Smokes, in certain stages of their kittenhood, but if the small signs that are characteristic of a Smoke kitten (as noted before) are not present at birth, they will be Black adults. These Blacks are not usually used in further breeding for Blacks but are valuable for use in future Smoke breedings.

Blue Smokes appear in Black-to-Smoke breedings, if there is also a Blue present behind the Black. The Blues that appear in these litters serve the same purpose in the furtherance of Blue Smoke breedings as do the Blacks from Smokes.

Smokes at the Show and at Home

Smokes usually do not attain their full beauty of coat until late December or January, and are not generally shown to good

Black Smoke female (right) owned by Orma Tillitson: SKYWAY'S STAR BABY (at 5 months of age). Sire: Ch. Kerry Lu Smoke Gem of Skyway; dam: Westbrook Sprite of Evergreen. Bred by V. V. Schuh.

Shaded Silver male (left) owned by Orma Tillitson: TR. CH. SKYWAY'S SILVER CUPID. Sire: Tr. Ch. Skyway's Stargazer; dam: Lowood's Mi-Honey Belle of Skyway. Bred by V. V. Schuh.

Black Smoke male owned by Mrs. Zelah Rush: DBL. CH. ANGELITA STORMY OF CRESTVIEW. Sire: Quad Ch. Kerry Lu Smoke Gem; dam: Miss Melinda of Angelita. Bred by Mrs. Pauline Frankenfield. Photo by Hans Bomskow.

advantage before that time. Even then, they are at their best for only a few months. They are not at their best when starting to shed, either, as both the top coat and the undercoat come out. There is more tendency for tabby markings to appear on the face and legs. The undercoat loses its whiteness, becoming gray, and the light ruff departs. It is helpful to keep your Smoke out of the strong sunlight as his new coat comes in to avoid a red, or sunburnt, tinge to the black topcoat.

Smokes of both colors have been creating much interest recently, and they certainly deserve it, for there is nothing quite as beautiful as a Smoke of good color and type. An excellent Smoke is one that will be admired by all.

The disposition of Smokes is extremely affectionate. They desire human companionship and love to sit in your lap. They often prefer one person above all others. I know of one stud that may be handled like a kitten, all eighteen pounds of him! I have fallen in love with several Smoke kittens I have met. Even though they are very sweet-tempered, they are independent, as all cats can be when up to some mischief or playing a cat game among themselves.

XXIV

CAMEO PERSIANS

Breeders from East and West, from North and South, from Canada, Australia, and New Zealand are exploring the possibilities of the tinsel-pink beauty of the newly recognized Persian color described as Cameo. Wherever it is benched, the Cameo Persian attracts attention, and a good specimen wins admiration from judges, exhibitors, and the general cat-loving public.

What Is Meant by "Cameo Coloring"

This new color is eye-catching. Each hair shades from ivory,

Shell Cameo male owned and bred by Mrs. A. D. Fergus: R.M. GR. CH. FERGUS'S HONEY BEAR. Sire: R. M. Gr. Ch. Fergus's Ginger Bear; dam: Chatami Cinderella. Photo by Clyde Powell.

white, or off-white next to the skin, to a soft cream or deep red at the tip. As in the case of the Silvers, the intensity of the tipping varies from one part of the cat to another. On the underparts, it is hardly present at all; on the back and the top of the tail, it shows up like a sparkling veil. The darker face is framed by an off-white neck ruff. Being a tipped cat, like the Silver, the Cameo may be very pale Shell (corresponding to the Chinchilla), Shaded Cameo (like the Shaded Silver) or Smoke Cameo (heavily tipped like the Black or Blue Smoke). Just imagine a smoke or silver coat in which the darker parts are cream or red instead of black, and you have the Cameo. Eye color for all Cameos is copper.

Note that the Cameo is not a new longhair breed, like the Himalayan, but only a new color in the Persian breed. It was first developed, intensively and deliberately, at Vanaki Cattery, Milton Junction, Wisconsin. Although over a period of twenty-odd years the owner had noted "pink" male kittens in various litters from a Smoke-Tortie crossing, she did not settle down to serious development of the color until 1954. The color, called Cameo because of the effect of its combination of white with cream and red, has now been standardized to the fiftieth generation—although even third generation Cameos will breed true.

Cameo and Cameo-Recessive Kittens

In the life of a Cameo kitten, the most critical moment is the one in which his owner recognizes the new kitten for what he is—a Cameo—instead of quickly concluding that he is a poor Red or a poor Cream. Actually, Cameos don't look at all like Creams or Reds, not even on the day they are born. Right on the back, perhaps, they may; but the little heads are almost white, and the underparts will be much lighter than the backs, just as with new-born Silvers. By the time they are two weeks old the whitish undercoat will show, even on the back, if you blow the hair gently. As a kitten grows, the specific Cameo color pattern begins to emerge, lighter for Shell, darker for Shaded, and holding deep dark for Smoke, with the face and forepaws growing redder and redder. Eye color in Smoke Cameos will be deeper than in Shells or Shaded Cameos. Little by little, the kitten's development lets you know what he may be expected to become.

In the litter which results from the first cross toward Cameos, there may be some females that are not Cameos but are of great genetic importance to the person who wishes to breed Cameos. They will be Silvers or Smokes, with cream or red patches distributed in Tortie fashion—split faces, cream toes, etc. They may properly be called Smoke-Creams or Silver-Creams. They are not monstrosities; they are Cameo recessives (genotypes). They carry the Cameo gene, although the color does not show in their coats, and at least one kitten in each of their litters will be Cameo, no matter what color male they are bred to, even a Black, Blue or White. These two-toned beauties are transmitters of Cameo color just as legitimately as the Tortoiseshell is a transmitter of Black or Red. Regardless of the fact that they cannot at this time be entered in a cat show profitably, you may wish to use them to expedite your getting directly to the Cameo (phenotype) kitten.

Shaded Cameo male owned by Mr. A. D. Fergus and bred by Mrs. A. D. Fergus: R.M. GR. CH. FERGUS'S GINGER BEAR. Sire: H.M. Gr. Ch. Fergus's Prince Juba; dam: Chatami Babette of Fergus. Photo by Clyde Powell.

Smoke Cameo male owned and bred by Pearl R. Allison: GR. CH. GIL-
MORE'S CAMEO SAM. Sire: Quad. Ch. Clairedale's Davy Crockett of
Gilmore; dam: Gilmore's Goldie. Photo by Gilman.

How to Start Breeding for Cameos

RULE: Breed any Silver or Smoke (these carry the shaded gene)
to any Red, Cream, or Tortoiseshell (Red-Cream gene), and you
can get at least one Cameo kitten in the litter.

Specific variations of the foregoing rule, together with indication of probable results, follow:

1. Mate a male from the Silver division to a female from the
Tabby and Tortie division, and the chances are high that
you will get a Cameo male.

2. Mate a female from the Silver division to a Cream or Red
male, and chances are high that you'll get one or more
Cameo females.

3. Mate any first-generation Cameo male to any first-generation Cameo female, and the chances are very high that the
litter will be comprised of seventy-five percent Cameos.

4. Mate any two Cameos of the second generation, and all
their kittens will be Cameos.

5. You may expect Cameos if the two necessary genetic factors (see RULE) are present one or two generations back.
For example: a White cat mated to a Blue-Cream produced a beautiful Cameo, because the White male's father
was a Smoke.

Breeders' Experiences

Every cattery owner owes himself the pleasure of raising at least one Cameo. They are beginning to be shown now, particularly in the Midwest and in the northern part of the West Coast. As many as eight or ten have been entered in a single show. In May, 1959, the Cameo Cat Club of America was formed to promote the breeding and exhibiting of the Cameo, and it now has members in widespread areas of the country, all of whom are pooling their experiences in the bi-monthly *Courier* sent to members.

The following are excerpts from Barbara Fergus's experience in the breeding of Cameos:

"They are the most lustrous of colors. The three shades—Shell, Shaded, and Smoke—could never be obtained without the beautiful Silver in their backgrounds. The type that is obtainable through the solid colors makes Cameos easy to breed for this feature, but we have the same problems of obtaining even shading as do Silver breeders.

"I have found the Cameo personality exceptional. Their temperament is good. They are easily handled and shown, and are very affectionate.

"There have been many picturesque words used to describe Cameo color, but, to me, they are vanilla ice cream, topped with orange sherbert. My most beautifully colored Cameos, to date, have come from a female that is a Silver-Cream cross, bred to a male of any color. I prefer males with Silver in their backgrounds.

"A sample of the results of my breeding is as follows:
Blue-Cream Female to Black Smoke Male resulted in two
    Tortie females, two Shaded Cameo males, one Blue male.
Silver-Cream-cross female to Shaded Cameo male (from
    above) resulted in three Shell Cameo males, one Shaded
    Cameo male, and one Blue female.
Blue-Cream female to Shell Cameo male (from above)
    resulted in two Blue-Cream females and a solid Red male
    (although there was no known Red in the previous
    pedigree).
"Sometimes, the shadings obtained from the Blue-Cream

have a tendency toward a cream tipping, which, while a beautiful color, when placed next to the luster of the red tips, cannot compare. However, these males and females, in turn, produce the true Cameo color, so they, too, are worth keeping.

"I've profited all around by getting out of the breeding rut I was in for years. My Torties are appearing with lovely color and excellent type. I had good resulting Smokes (a color I'd been trying to improve for some time) by using my Shaded Cameo, Ch. Ginger Bear. He was from Blue-Cream and Black Smoke parentage. Breeding him to my color-bred Smoke female, I got Smokes with short cobby bodies, thick chests, short heavy legs, and true white under-coat and black top-coat, plus Blue type."

XXV
THE MOSAIC PATTERN

The word *tabis*, in French, means the "silken one." A certain quarter of old Baghdad was called Attabbiah. Here they made a special type of black and white silk with a watered effect, similar to the "moire" pattern seen in material. When this silk from Attabbiah was imported to England and France, it was commonly called Tabbi-silk. Someone then saw a likeness between the stripes and watermarks of this silk and the bars and butterflies of the coat of a certain cat, which came to be called a "Tabbi-cat," later shortened to Tabby.

Tabby Markings

Perfect Tabby markings are highly desirable, but seldom seen,

Red Tabby female owned by Paul Reid: **CH. ELCO'S TAMMY.** Sire: Elco's Major Markwell; dam: Cheney's Sugar Cookie. Bred by Ella Conroy.

as there almost always is some variation, particularly from one side of the cat to the other.

Starting with the head, the desired pattern of markings for all Tabby colors is as follows:

There should be several sets of matching stripes on the face. The stripes on the forehead sometimes form an "M." The lines between the ears extend down to the nose in front, continuing over the back of the head and neck. The cheeks are barred with lines that start from the outer corner of each eye giving the effect of spectacles. These lines, or whorls, curve toward the back of the head, following the contours of the cheek.

The lines on the back, alongside the spine, are a continuation of the head markings. These "spinals" consist of a single stripe down the back, with another one on either side of it, separated by a width of ground color approximately the same thickness as the stripes.

Over each shoulder and along each side are markings that form a circle (on the shoulder) and an oval (on the side). These have circles and ovals within themselves and a solid "eye" in the center, like a target. The perfection of these markings is dependent not only on their circular contour but also on the spacing and evenness of their width and the width of the intervening ground color. There should be no hair of the ground color mixed into the "eyes" or any of the markings.

If the back and sides of the coat were removed and laid flat, the whole pattern of markings would resemble a swallowtail butterfly.

The front and hind legs are evenly barred, giving the effect of bracelets. The bars should come up high on the legs to meet the body markings. The chest and neck should have wide bands of color, like so many necklaces, each solid, separate, and distinct from the other, stopping at the spine lines and "butterfly" marking of the shoulders and sides.

The tail should be evenly ringed, ending with a dark tip not much wider than the other rings.

The belly fur is all of the ground color, but dotted with evenly spaced solid round marks, or "buttons."

The effect of these markings is striking, and one finds a fascination in tracing these lines and patterns. The more contrast there is between the dark color of the markings and the lighter tone of the ground color, the more outstanding the markings are. In their perfection, they look as though they were drawn or painted on by the hand of a master draftsman.

A Tabby Is Groomed to Show Off His Markings

A Tabby is groomed for show differently from other Persians. As half of the points allotted to color are given for markings in Tabbies, it is most important that the Tabby be combed to show up its markings. If the hair is combed and fluffed out from the body too much, the markings are diffused; therefore, instead of combing and brushing the hair to stand out from the body as is done with the Persians of other colors, the hair should be combed down flat, the way the coat grows, to define and accentuate the markings. For this reason, it has sometimes been said that Tabbies do not have the same coat length as other Persians, which, of course, is not true. Powder should not be used, as it would dim the markings. A touch of coat conditioner will help the coat to lie flat, as well as impart shine and gloss to the markings which make the properly groomed Tabby a beautiful sight.

When the two longhair strains, Persian and Angora, began to be blended with the objective of working toward the Persian-type head and body, there were so few Persian Tabbies, as mentioned before, that the Tabby breeders were unable to cross to Persian with their Angora Tabbies the same way as the other colors were crossed.

In nature, the more common tabby-type markings are the indistinct and diffused "mackerel tabby," or tiger-striped. Those interested in breeding Tabbies felt that a distinct pattern of swirls and wide bands would be more interesting and attractive. In order to develop this unusual pattern they had to breed together Tabbies with tendencies toward the desired markings. This put the Tabby breeders somewhat behind in their progress toward heavier, shorter bodies, wider heads, and smaller, rounded ears. After their Tabby patterns were set, they then were able to breed to the solid-color Persians to develop better type.

The breeding procedures for the various colors of Tabby Persian are different, but the requirements of contrast and the pattern itself are exactly the same for all.

XXVI

SILVER TABBY PERSIANS

The Silver Tabby Personality

Silver Tabby cats are extroverts. They have an outgoing and affectionate personality and desire their owner's companionship above all else. They delight in following you around the house, carrying on a conversation in a quiet, loving voice. They are mischievous and fun-loving and make unbelievably wonderful pets for a family with children or for people who want a cat that thinks he is a person.

Silver Tabby female owned and bred by Dorothy Baker: R.M. TR. CH. YOUR PET'S MEESE. Sire: R.M. Gr. Ch. Your Pet's Moose; dam: Ch. Phil-Bet's Jemara of Your Pets. Photo by John White.

Silver-Markings

Silver Tabbies are strikingly beautiful cats, with pitch black markings standing out on a pale-silver coat. Their face markings give them an appealing pansy-like face, and their expressions are sweet, like the Silvers'. They, as do the Silvers, have eyes outlined with black, as if with mascara, brick-red noses outlined in black, and the coat's ground color is a light silver tipped with black, exactly the same as the coat of the Silvers. Overlaid on top of this silver coat is the specific pattern of markings, which should be as black as possible. The overall appearance is similar to a beautiful mosaic. Their eyes are green or hazel. The green eye color is preferable, and much work is being done to improve it.

Difficulties in the Breeding of Silver Tabbies

Mrs. Don Martin, of Silver Sword Cattery, tells of her experiences with Silver Tabbies:

"One step forward and two backward sums up the difficulties facing the breeder of this fascinating cat. Genetically, the Silver Tabby is a tremendous challenge, but perhaps the most interesting and rewarding of all the Persian varieties to breed successfully. Stubbornness and perseverance are the most important attributes of a Silver Tabby breeder; it's like chasing four kittens—named Type, Eye Color, Tipped Undercoat, and Markings. You can catch only one at a time, and while you are holding one in each hand, you watch the other two disappear under the bed!

"You cannot breed Silver Tabby to Silver Tabby generation after generation and keep the clear definition of black upon silver, nor can you keep the very distinct markings from reverting to the mackerel or blotched markings. The tone of the face markings will become lighter than the body marks. Also, another fault which comes from breeding Silver Tabby to Silver Tabby *ad infinitum* is a definite loss of type.

"Selective breeding, using a Black and Silver cross, is the best way to breed for Silver Tabbies. The cross with a top-quality Black is an excellent way to improve both the depth

244

of the markings and the type of the Tabby. A Black with some, but not too much, Blue in its background is the best. When crossing this way, however, two things must be kept in mind: first, the Silver Tabby's green eye color will be masked with the dominant copper eye color of the Black, for the first generation; and, second, it will then require careful breeding back to the Chinchilla, Shaded, or Tabby Silvers to restore the green eyes without diluting the improved markings that have been achieved.

"A good plan is to first cross a very dark Silver Tabby with a Chinchilla or a Shaded Silver and, at the same time, an excellent type Black with a Silver Tabby who has better-than-average type, and then mate the children of these two crosses together. By doing this, good type, ground color, and markings, and also reasonably good green eye color, should be obtained in two generations.

"Another plan is a cross of a good-type Blue-Eyed White with a background of some Blue or Black. The White will keep the silver ground coat clear, without any brown tinge, and give you the same excellent type and dark markings of the Black cross.

"Using a Blue-Eyed White will not, in most cases, mask the green eye color quite as much as does a Black cross; often, it will produce a reasonable greenish-hazel eye color. Another thing to remember concerning eye color is the slowness of its development in the Silver Tabby. It sometimes takes two years, or slightly more, for the hazel eye to develop into a good green eye. If you have a good solid-green rim around the iris of the eye in your eight-month-old kitten, you can be pretty confident that the kitten will have good green eyes at between two and three years of age. Of course, if this green rim has yellow mixed in with it, you will end up with only a hazel eye color.

"When I recommend a Black or White without a predominance of Blue in the background, I do so because I have found a cross with a color-bred Blue can produce a "Brown" Tabby or will impart a definite cream and brown tinge to the Silver Tabby coat.

Silver Tabby male owned and bred by Mrs. Donald Martin: CH. SILVER SWORD'S VALENTINO. Sire: Quint. Ch. Willow Mist's Tobermory; dam: Tr. Ch. Marleon Fur Fun Merrilegs. Photo by Muzzie.

"When a Brown Tabby appears in Silver Tabby breeding, it usually has green eyes, excellent type, and very good markings, and thus a breeder may be tempted to reason that it is a good cat to breed back again to the Silver Tabby. Such reasoning is erroneous. Granted, here is a cat with a Silver Tabby background and good type, but it is also a cat bearing the dominant genes for Brown Tabby coloring and carrying the Silver Tabby coloring only as a recessive. If you breed this Brown Tabby back in, you are increasing the chances of its dominant Brown Tabby strain appearing again and again, both as Brown Tabbies and as the fault of cream or brown mixed in your silver coat, when you want Silver Tabbies. Once bred in, this trait is practically impossible to breed out again.

Silver Tabbies Are Nearly Black When Born

"When Silver Tabby kittens are born, they are very black, with only a little of the silver ground coat showing through to give you an idea of what the adult markings will be. The darker the markings at birth, the better the markings will be in the grown cat. Most Silver Tabby kittens do not, at first glance, seem to have the three necessary spinal markings, but if you will put your kittens under a strong light, you will see a faint shadow on either side of the center spinal line, denoting the silver ground coat that will come through as they grow older. The markings of a kitten at birth are the markings of the adult. If a Silver Tabby kitten is not nearly black with very dominant markings at the time of birth, it will turn into a poorly marked adult.

"It is desirable to pick the type of the Silver Tabby kitten between four to five weeks of age, because after this time it can go through some extremely awkward stages in which the ears sit on top of the head, the nose looks much too long, and the body gets rangy and loses the appearance of cobbiness. In other words, it looks like the adolescent child —all out of proportion. One of the hardest things in Silver Tabby breeding is to be patient and hold onto your faith while a kitten goes through these growing pains. It is necessary to remember that no matter what a Tabby looks like at five and six months, it will revert to the type it had when five weeks old. However, the tendency to go through these awkward stages generally makes it extremely difficult to show them in the kitten class.

Silver Tabby female owned and bred by Mr. and Mrs. Don Martin: R.M. GR. CH. and QUINT. CH. SILVER SWORD'S FILIGREE. Sire: Tr. Ch. Sir Pepper of Silver Vista; dam: Tr. Ch. Marleon Fur Fun Merrilegs. Photo by Don Martin.

When a Silver-Tabby Looks Like a Shaded Silver

"A Silver Tabby also goes through some disconcerting coat changes during the shedding season. As he sheds his coat, the markings either disappear to the point where you think you have a Shaded Silver, or the spinal markings stay and all the other markings on the flanks, tail, and chest disappear. There is no need to worry. As the new coat comes in, so do the markings. Heat will cause markings to fade, and a Silver Tabby shown in the period from August through October rarely will display his best black markings or the length of coat found in most of the solid colors; the Tabbies are generally late-coaters. Another thing to watch out for is strong sunlight during the summer months, for it will make the markings turn rusty or brownish.

"The popularity of this beautiful color variety has increased tremendously within the last few years, and there are many more excellent Silver Tabbies appearing in the shows now than in previous years. The greater interest being shown should help considerably in producing a Silver Tabby with outstanding type and markings."

XXVII

RED TABBY PERSIANS

Red is the most popular color of Tabby, particularly in the Middle West. However, Red Tabby coloring is such that it is the most difficult in which to obtain enough contrast. The markings are just a deep shade of red on a light-red base color. Unless these markings are very deep and on a base coat which is considerably lighter, they do not show up as well as when an entirely different color is superimposed on a base coat. If a Red Tabby has a long coat, the markings blend in with the base coat even more.

Tabby markings, as prescribed, require the distinct separation of the "spinals," or back stripes. The side stripes on a Red Tabby often are inclined to merge or be joined with the center one. Also, Red Tabbies are inclined to have a light tip to their tails (in earlier days, they often had a white tail tip).

Red Tabby Breeding Tips

Pauline Frankenfield, of Angelita Cattery, gives us this information about Red Tabby breeding:

"Red Tabbies are usually color-bred cats, with only an occasional outcross being made to another color. In their breeding, Red Tabby to Red Tabby will strengthen both color and markings. They can be bred to a Blue for type improvements or to a Cream to try for better color contrasts. Breeding to a solid Red will lessen the markings. A Black is not recommended as a cross, as it will muddy the red color, but a cat which is a combination of Red and Black can be used. A Tortoiseshell, for instance, can be used to good advantage, particularly if she herself has a Red Tabby in her ancestry. A shorter nose and face can be obtained from crossbreeding with the Peke-Faced Red Tabby, but this cross also may produce a tendency toward longer

Red Tabby female kitten owned by Mr. and Mrs. Jack Hale: ANJAC'S ANJOU. Sire: Gr. Ch. Jer-I-Mey Escamillo of Anjac; dam: Gr. Ch. Far-Fin Lola of Anjac. Photo by Don Martin.

ears. Other common faults to avoid in Red Tabbies are too-short fur length and too-long tails."

How to Pick a Red Tabby Kitten

Mrs. John Hunter, who has had a long-time interest in both Red Tabbies and Torties, tells us how to pick a Red Tabby kitten:

"As the kitten is marked at birth and for a few days after, so will it be marked as an adult. If the spine lines are absent then, they will not come later. The markings of a Red Tabby kitten often fade out for a while, but the permanent color and markings begin to set when the kitten reaches six months of age."

Ideal Red Tabby Coloring

Mrs. Hunter describes the ideal Red Tabby color as being comparable to the clear, sparkling, mahogany shade of the Irish Setter dog. The eye color should be near to that same depth for the greatest beauty. Her Eastbury Trigo had this coloring and was a very well known winner in his time.

The Red Tabby Personality

Red Tabbies can be a bit peppery, but they also can be very sweet and devotedly loyal to their owners. Red Tabbies are seen in their most beautiful aspect when in the sunlight, particularly when walking or lying on a green lawn.

XXVIII

PEKE-FACED PERSIANS

There are only two colors of Peke Faces, Red and Red Tabby, now recognized for show in the United States. None is eligible in England. These are cats whose faces resemble that of the Pekingese dog. They have a very short pug nose and a slight indentation at the "break" where the nose meets the forehead. There is a wrinkle running from the inside corner of the eye to the outside corner of the mouth.

Their eyes are set so that they appear to "pop" out. The forehead often curves outward, creating a sort of bulge that has

Red Tabby Peke-faced female owned by Mr. and Mrs. Jack Hale: GR. CH. FAR-FIN LOLA OF ANJAC. Sire: Gr. Ch. Elco Rudolpho; dam: Far-Fin Violetta. Bred by Farris and Fincel. Photo by Don Martin.

another indentation above it. In a true Peke Face, this dent may be felt with your fingers. Some of the Pekes have deformities of the jaw, being slightly undershot, and they often have protruding teeth. These faults are not desirable, but to get a Peke with perfect jaw and teeth alignment is rare. It is objectionable if the teeth do not meet evenly in the "bite."

The general face conformation and eye color usually is good, with the exception of the problem that is common to all colors —size and placement of the ears. Where breeders of other colors may breed selectively to overcome this fault, the breeders of Peke-Faced cats do not have much opportunity to do so.

Red Tabby Peke Face

Peke Faces, apparently, occur spontaneously in litters of Reds and Red Tabbies. Among the solid Reds, Peke Faces are seen less often than among the Red Tabbies. This, no doubt, is due to the fact that the solid Reds themselves are less numerous than Red Tabbies.

Peke Faces bred to other Peke Faces do not necessarily produce Peke Faces. There is no pattern to use to consistently produce them, much less be able to breed for individual features that need to be improved upon. The color and marking requirements for Peke Faces are the same as for the standard type. A good type, and well-marked, deep-colored Red or Red Tabby Peke Face is a comparative rarity, due to the inherent limitations of their breeding. Gr. Ch. Jer-I-Mey Escamillo of Anjac is one of this variety that has been awarded top show honors in recent years.

Marie Williams, of Colonial Cattery, has contributed some notes on Pekes from her own experiences and those of other Peke breeders:

"It has been said that the Peke Face appears as a quirk of nature. This has been true in my experience. I have bred a full Peke-Face male to a full Peke-Face female, and from that union only Standard Red Tabbies appeared. I have bred standard Red Tabby to Standard Red Tabby and all their kittens were Pekes. Appearing in one litter from Standard Red Tabby parents, there was a top show-type Peke-Face

Red Tabby Peke-faced male owned by Mr. and Mrs. Jack Hale: GR. CH. JER-I-MEY ESCAMILLO OF ANJAC. Sire: Gr. Ch. Colonial's King Peter; dam: Dbl. Gr. Ch. Far-Fin Mignon of Jer-i-Mey. Bred by Meyers. Photo by Don Martin.

female, and also an equally fine type Standard Red Tabby female. It is sometimes hard to tell whether a kitten will be a Peke or a Standard Red Tabby. I had one male that did not develop his Peke head until he was six months old.

"In breeding for Red Tabby Pekes you seem to have the following situation: you either get a good Peke head and poor markings or good markings and a poor Peke head. The distinctive feature about any Peke, however, is his head, so we try more for good head type and hope for the markings.

"Breeders of Standard Red Tabbies like to have a Peke somewhere in the background of their line because of their short face and nose. Cream Pekes have resulted from Red and Cream breeding. Pekes are also known to appear from other color breedings. There is no color class for these cats at present, but if they become more numerous it may be possible for them to be recognized as a separate variety.

"There is a high mortality rate in Pekes at birth and in kittens up to six months old. The most hardy Peke kittens seem to come from parents who have some standard Persian in the background. Peke kittens are hard to raise, but as they remain babies much longer this gives you additional time to enjoy them. Many mothers will nurse and take care of their kittens until they are five months old.

"Peke cats and kittens are very agile. They have great power in their hind legs and use them to kick and fight like a rabbit does. Their nails are extremely hooked and can dig into anything. They like to jump to your shoulder. This can be quite painful if you are wearing light clothing! They often eat with their paws and even drink water that way. I have seen them pull the food plate entirely away from the other cats with their paws and the other cats be powerless to get it back. They are very jealous; I have even had them nudge our little dog off my lap when they wanted attention.

"They seem to to be a one-person cat and usually like men better than women. The female Pekes especially seem to prefer men. If a person has ever had a Peke or a litter of Peke kittens, they will always want another, as they are certainly different and interesting."

XXIX

BLUE TABBY PERSIANS

I am indebted to Mrs. Thomas Martinke for the description of, and information concerning, the breeding of Blue Tabby Persians contained in the following:

The Blue Tabby is a true Tabby, wholly distinct, and not to be confused with any other color. Silver Tabbies and Brown Tabbies are like a full symphony with their rich, strong backgrounds and bold, black striping. The Blue Tabbies might be likened to a Chopin nocturne in their delicacy and delight. The standard adopted for them describes them literally and clearly, but cannot possibly convey the sense of their charm, the shimmering "ashes of roses" patina over their basic color, or the wonderful harmony of their color pattern. The standard is as follows:

Ground color, including lips and chin, pale bluish ivory with warm fawn overtones, fawn more noticeable on upper part of face. Markings very deep blue, affording good con-

Blue Tabby female owned by Mrs. C. A. Coughlin: JENK'S SUDDENLY OF CO-MC. Bred by Mr. and Mrs. H. L. Jenkins.

trast with ground color. Pattern of markings as described for Brown Tabbies. Lips and chin slightly lighter in kittens and young adults. Nose leather, rose. Eyes, copper or deep orange, copper preferred.

Throughout the years, most breeders doing intensive work with Brown Tabbies have experienced the phenomenon of the appearance of Blue Tabbies in the Brown Tabby litters when the pedigrees seem to offer no reason for it. Such kittens have always had a much more intensive copper eye color than their Brown Tabby brothers and sisters.

It is now almost a certainty that the Blue Tabbies which appear in this way are true spontaneous dilutions of the basic Brown Tabby, and bear the same relationship thereto that a Blue Point Siamese does to a Seal Point. Thus they are a true color, which in time may be established as strongly in their own right as the Blue Point Siamese already have been. Unfortunately, it will take longer to accomplish this, since there are comparatively few breeders working with the Brown Tabbies, whereas there are many Siamese breeders. Certain bloodlines seem to carry a stronger gene for this dilution than others, so that when they are combined, or there is inbreeding or linebreeding in them, a much greater proportion of Blue Tabbies will result. In one recent litter from well-known Brown Tabbies, where seventeen of the first thirty ancestors were Brown Tabbies and no Blue was included closer than the great-grandparents, the proportion of Blue Tabbies in the litter was four to one.

Blue Tabby is a true color created by nature, but there is another interesting facet in that it may also be created artificially by crossing Brown Tabby and Blue. It has always been known that the introduction of Black into Brown Tabby bloodlines for one generation will help to clarify and deepen the markings which may have been showing a tendency to become muddy, indistinct, and ticked. In recent years, many of the best Brown Tabby breeders have been crossing their Brown Tabbies very carefully with Blues to improve the type of Brown with as little loss of intensity of markings as possible. These crosses resulted in a great many that were well marked in the first generation.

Few cats other than Blues have ever had a specific role to play in the improvement of another color, but a few hardy souls among the Brown breeders kept some of the better Blue Tabbies, even though they were AOC (Any Other Color), because they well knew that some of the best and most perfectly marked Brown Tabbies could be produced from them.

Just recently, the Blue Tabby has been recognized for championship status. Happily, the recognition of this color is a two-fold blessing. At one and the same time, it gives to the fancy a new and striking color which is as beautiful as any of the longer-established ones, and provides a most effective means for rapid improvement of the Brown Tabbies (so dear to the hearts of their admirers and especially those who remember them in their hey-day when they could hold their own in competition with the colors which now dominate the top wins at our shows). This recognition, though, is a beginning, not an ending, and much work remains to be done with this fascinating new color. A great deal of experimentation is needed to determine just what proportions of the various colors will produce the strongest combination of type and markings. This is a task to which the Tabby breeder must apply himself.

Blue Tabbies today are not a Blue cat with darker markings, tickings or shadings. Such cats as these are simply flawed Blues which should never be mistaken for Blue Tabbies, whose basic ground color is a blued old-ivory. This color is particularly evident on the underside, where the ground color may be seen in larger areas. The true Blue Tabby must have those face markings which lend such piquancy to all Tabby faces. The rings around their eyes and the chin and lip area are a very pale, cool ivory. Any cat whose face or underside is blue may automatically be eliminated as a Blue Tabby show cat.

XXX

BROWN TABBY PERSIANS

There is something about a Brown Tabby that makes people say, "There's a cat that looks exactly *like* a cat!" They are a very handsome variety of Persian. The Tabby pattern of markings is very effective in itself. On the Brown Tabby, they are jet black painted on a warm brown base coat. The swirls and stripes of their face markings add to their "smiling" expressions. Brown Tabbies beam good will at you. They are usually medium

Brown Tabby male and Brown Tabby female owned by Mrs. Dorothy B. Anderson. DBL. CH. SUNNYLAND BROWN ROBIN OF JAY KAY, JAY KAY GEE GEE. Sire: Ch. Light Wing Nehra of Sunnyland; dam: Ch. Sunnyland Levinnia; dam: Ch. Mil-War's Cherakee Sherry.

Brown Tabby male owned and bred by Mr. and Mrs. James Elliott: QUAD. CH. GLENN-LYN DON TOMAS. Sire: Gatilo Oro El Trobador; dam: Silver Vista Peachy Miss. Photo by Gordon Laughner.

to large in size, but are like overgrown kittens with their playful natures. A Brown Tabby never grows up, and seldom do you hear a cross word from him, unless he is greatly provoked.

Mr. Phil Jacobs, of Mar-Vista Cattery, made the study of cat genetics his life-work. He found the color inheritance pattern of the Brown Tabby particularly interesting and specialized in their breeding. His conclusions have given invaluable help to breeders of all colors who had the opportunity to hear his lectures, particularly to Mrs. James Elliott of Glen-Lyn, who has followed his principles in her work with the "Brownies." Some pointers from her experience are in the following paragraphs.

They are often mated to Reds or Red Tabbies to intensify the warm tawny tones of brown that are called for in their base coloring. They are also mated to Blacks to improve type and to keep the blackness of their tabby markings. The usual procedure

Brown Tabby female owned by Eugenia Elliott : DBL. CH. SILVER VISTA PEACHY MISS OF GLEN LYN. Sire: Kiva Chieftan of Silver Vista; dam: Blu Ballerina of Silver Vista. Bred by Elissa Elser. Photo by Gordon Laughner.

in their breeding, however, is for a Brown Tabby to be mated to another Brown Tabby. The brown coloring is dominant, so it is strengthened by this type of breeding. In nature, apparently, Brown base color and Black markings somehow are linked, as this is a common color pattern in all varieties of domestic cats. Also, these colors, although lighter and marked to a lesser degree, are found in wild cats.

When a Brown Tabby female has Red or Red Tabby in her background, as is common, she carries the red color gene. Regardless of what color cat she is mated to, she will have at least one (and usually two) kitten that shows the red color factor in the form of a Red, Red Tabby, or even a Cameo. Apparently, the Brown Tabby males genetically are Brown Tabbies, and a Brown Tabby male anywhere in a pedigree will cause Brown Tabbies to appear, very unexpectedly in some cases, with great regularity.

Brown Tabby breeders have the same problems of trying to overcome deficiencies of type that are common to all Tabby colors. Breeding to Blues with some Black ancestors, producing the Blue Tabby as an intermediate, may solve this problem.

The Brown Tabby's markings are most effective when he has a comparatively short, plushy coat, the type which shows off markings beautifully. Unfortunately, such a cat usually is penalized for coat length in the judging. The longer the coat, however, the less evident the markings. A fault that once was quite common in Brown Tabbies was that fur on the chin was white. This tendency has been overcome in recent years, and if the chin appears to be nearly white, the color should be checked at the skin, where the true color can be determined. The color of the base coat on the face often is a lighter shade of brown than that on the body, particularly around the eyes and mouth. The color of the chin fur should match this tone.

The true potential of a Brown Tabby kitten cannot be determined until he is about four months old. When a tawny, rich ground color is present on a young kitten, he probably will have

Brown Tabbies owned and bred by Dottie Woods.

**Brown Tabby female owned by Mrs. A. C. Oliver: CO-MC'S TAWNEY.
Bred by Mrs. C. A. Coughlin. Photo by Abrams.**

good ground color as an adult. The black markings sometimes appear rusty, but they can deepen and develop. Many kittens that are too heavily marked, or whose heavy markings have blurred outlines, will have clear markings of the proper width as they grow older.

XXXI

TORTOISESHELL PERSIANS

A boldly marked Tortoiseshell is a striking Persian. Some look as if they were wearing masquerade dresses. Their coloring was likened to that of some tortoises, which is how they came to be designated Tortoiseshell. This tortoiseshell pattern of coat colors appears quite frequently in the domestic cats. Tortoiseshell coloring has long been considered attractive by many persons, and Torties were known to exist with either long or short coats long before there were any shows or breeding for color was attempted. Early Torties and Torties with White quite likely were the results of natural breedings. They were highly valued by those who had them, for they usually produced Tortie kittens like themselves, as well as those of other colors.

Torties can be produced deliberately by breeding a Red Persian to a Black or Blue Persian. However, Torties from a Blue mating will go off-color earlier in the year, when the undercoat takes on a bluish tinge. This does not conform to the standard and for show purposes must be stripped out. Red Tabbies, too, will produce Tortoiseshells, if bred to Black, but this will bring out undesirable ticking and bars in the color patches.

The distribution of the three colors—black, red, and cream—which constitute a Tortoiseshell should be as equal as possible. However, one color, usually black, predominates. The patches of each color should have only that color of hair in the patch. Any intermingling of colors gives a blurred or brindled effect. The size of each patch, with the exception of the face markings, should not be large.

A "blaze," or streak of light color, down one side of the forehead and nose often is referred to in speaking of Torties.

Some associations require a blaze on a Tortoiseshell's face, and penalize for lack thereof. All associations consider the blaze a desirable feature. It may be either red or cream. Sometimes the entire chin is a light color. Even more striking is for half of the

Tortoiseshell female owned and bred by Dr. and Mrs. George F. Mayfield: **CH. SANDHILLS PAINTED MADONNA**. Sire: Dbl. Ch. Rocky Mountain Purring Tobias of Sandhills; dam: Dbl. Ch. Shawnee Dina of Sandhills.

Tortoiseshell female owned by Miss Annette Smith; GR. PR. SMITHWAY BERDINA. Sire: Lighwaing Warrior of Smithway; dam: Azulita Chi Baba of Smithway. Bred by Helen Smith. Photo by Gordon Laughner.

chin to be light, and on the opposite side of the blaze. A blaze is desirable on the face of a Blue Cream, too.

It has been noticed that although the standard requires that cream be on the back also, it seldom is present in any quantity. This tendency may tie up with the fact that the original protective coloring of animals always shows the lighter color underneath. Cream, being a dilute form of red, would be more likely to appear on the underside parts in greater quantity, with the red more predominate on top.

The feet of a Tortie should be patched. Again, the alternating design is most attractive. Most desirable is to have each foot so colored.

Those who like surprise and variety in a litter of kittens will find the breeding of and to Torties most interesting. They are

267

generally mated to males of any solid color, except white, and produce kittens of almost any color.

Fact and Fancy

Tortoiseshell coloring is sex-linked, as is also the Blue-Cream. Although occasionally a Tortoiseshell male appears, he is usually not fertile. Therefore, for all practical purposes, all Torties are females. The fallacy of a Tortie male being very valuable is one that has persisted through the years. In reality it would have no extra value except as a curiosity. This tale seems to have started in the time of Queen Victoria. Someone supposedly offered £100 (at that time approximately $500) to anyone who could produce a male of this color which could sire kittens.

Mrs. John Hunter has long been interested in Tortoiseshell cats and was instrumental in improving their quality in the United States. Her description is apt: "A black-painted fence, with splotches of red and cream thrown on it." Their eye color is copper or deep amber and is usually good.

Torties are invariably sweet cats and make very fine pets and wonderful, strong mothers.

XXXII

CALICO PERSIANS

Basically, a Calico Persian's coloring is the same as that of the tri-colored Tortoiseshell, the difference being the addition of white. In fact, they are sometimes called Tortie and White. Although it is a color pattern that has been in existence since the beginning of our records on cats, it has just recently become eligible for championship status in the United States. This recognition probably will increase the number of persons interested in their breeding and result in better specimens.

The Calico pattern is sex-linked to the female. It has the same requirements as the Tortoiseshell, except that its patching may be likened to a tri-colored coat and hat being worn over a white dress. The black, red, and cream splotches, each well defined, should cover the top of the head, ears, cheeks, back, tail, and parts of the flanks. Patches of each color should be distinct, clear of brindling or tabby markings. Deep orange or copper eyes are proper.

Results of the breeding of this color have attracted the attention of scientists interested in color inheritance. White is dominant over all other colors in cats. In Calico breeding, it is the hardest to breed out and the easiest to get more of. White spotting can, and does, happen in all colors of Persians. It is not known whether these white spots are a result of lack of pigment or, which is probably more likely in the breeding of the Calico Persian, a reversion to the original White Angora.

Mrs. Dorothy Anderson, of Jay-Kay Cattery, has bred this interesting color variety in conjunction with the so-called "Picture Cats" (the term applied to any solid color with white in an even pattern). "Picture Cats" are not recognized for show at this time, but are a part of Calico breeding. They are striking and worthy of attention for their own sake.

Mrs. Anderson shows the Calico pattern coming out in the fourth generation from different breeding combinations:

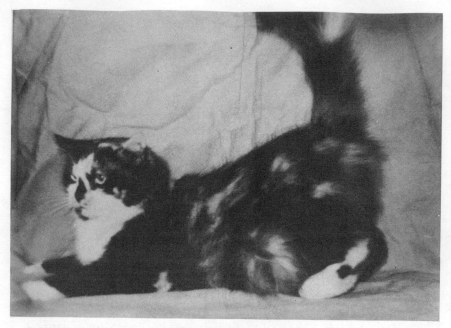

Calico female owned and bred by Dorothy B. Anderson: CH. JAY-KAY LADY CHECKERBOARD. Sire: Ch. Spero Sir George Bimbo; dam: Queen Patches of Jay Kay.

"The Black and White male or Red and White male is the masculine counterpart of a Calico. Breed a Tortie or Red Tabby to the Black and White male, and the Red and White male to a Tortie or Black female. Use a male with the best type and the least white, as the amount of white will increase in the kittens.

"The kittens that result may be Calicos or Torties, or Torties with just a little white, as well as solid color kittens, according to what breeding is behind the two parents.

"If you get a Calico on the first cross, this pattern will continue to come out in some of her kittens in the form of Calico females and Black and White or Red and White males, regardless of what further crosses you make with this Calico.

"Keep in mind that Blue will help the type, but may dilute the red to more cream than will be desired. Also, it will increase the amount of white.

"If you use the Tortie (or a Tortie with a little white) female for further pursuit of Calicos, she should be mated back to her sire."

White on the legs and breast is desirable, but too much white on the body is not. If any kitten appears that has the three colors and white (in any proportion), it is well to keep it, as the colors may spread further and develop with age. Sometimes the red and cream are difficult to distinguish on the coat of a young kitten, and what will later be black may be only a dull blue.

No white hair should appear in the other-colored patches.

Calico is a very charming variety of Persian, always scrupulously clean. The white area is always dazzling, showing off the "Joseph's Coat of Many Colors" wonderfully.

XXXIII

HYBRID LONGHAIRS

The Himalayan

The establishment and recognition of a new breed of cats is a rare achievement. In the United States, the originator of the Himalayan, a Siamese-Persian cross, was Mrs. Marguerita Goforth. She tells the story of this unusual accomplishment as follows:

"One article recently read states that the Himalayan is not a longhaired Siamese, but is a Persian. The first part of the

Chocolate point Himalayan male bred and owned by Mrs. J. F. Goforth: QUAD. CH. GOFORTH'S CHOCOLATE SOLDIER. Sire: Goforth's Sir Diamond; dam: Ch. Goforth's Winsome Lass. Photo by Gordon Laughner.

statement is quite correct, since we are breeding for a cobby Persian type with Siamese coloring only. The second part is in error, for the Himalayan is not a Persian. If it were, there could be no Siamese blood in it, and thus no Siamese color. No, the Himalayan is neither Siamese nor Persian but an entirely new breed of longhair. In other words, we now have two breeds of longhairs—Persians and Himalayans—just as we have several breeds of shorthairs, each of which is a distinct breed in itself, not a division of another breed.

"Many persons ask what is involved in originating a new breed such as the Himalayan. The answer is—many years of selective line-breeding, many cages, many cats, moments of discouragement, and times when the breeder wonders if it is worth the tremendous amount of work, expense, and worry. There are many discards because of poor type, wrong color, etc., for several generations, and homes for these must be found where they will not be used for breeding purposes. Then comes the final step and proof that you have actually originated a new breed. This is when official recognition by the cat association is achieved. Until one receives this official recognition, he has not developed a breed. Simple crosses do not make a breed. One thing, and only one thing, official recognition by the associations, makes a new breed a reality. This can only be accomplished when the cats conform to a type and breed true, and this takes years of breeding with a plan, a 'blueprint,' of what the ideal cat should be.

"Another question often asked is why I named this cat the Himalayan; sometimes, even, how did I import the original stock from Himalaya! I gave them this name because the color pattern is like that found in other animals, for example, the Himalayan rabbit, which has the same light body color and dark contrasting points. There were no imports, and the Himalayan developed slowly in my cattery over a period of nearly ten years.

"The standard for the Himalayan lays stress on type, but, in essence, it is as follows: Persian type, Siamese color, and blue eyes, the deeper the better. Undesirable and incorrect: any similarity in type to Siamese, eyes any color other than blue; kinked tails and crossed eyes are not allowed.

"The first kittens were either Seal Points or Blue Points, but now Chocolate Points and Lilac Points have appeared.

"In disposition, the Himalayan is 'the most,' very sweet and affectionate. The loud voice of the Siamese has been bred out, and the more genteel voice of the Persian has taken over. They are lively, alert, and intelligent, more like the Siamese in their antics."

Mrs. Goforth's Chocolate Soldier and her Mona Lisa are two of the first outstanding examples of her work to attain championship status.

Classification for color in Himalayans follows the standard for Siamese cats.

COLOR STANDARD FOR HIMALAYAN AND

COLOUR POINT LONG HAIRS

EYE COLOR: Clear and as deep blue as possible for the breed. Pale or slatey eyes to be discouraged.

BODY COLOR: In judging older cats, allowance should be made for darker coats, since they generally darken with age, but there should be a definite contrast between body color and points. Point allotment: Proper color, 4; proper shading, 4; evenness of color, 7; kittens lighter in color.

Blue point Himalayan male owned by A. D. Sketchley: CH. PERSEPOLIS HANNABAL. Sire: Tr. Ch. Sunnyside King Solomon of Persepolis; dam: Ch. Briarry Zulueta of Persepolis (Imp.). Bred by Corol MacMillan.

POINTS: Mask, ears, legs, feet and tail, dense and clearly defined, all of the same shade. Mask should be connected to the ears by tracings except in kittens. Point allotment: Mask, 2; Ears, 2; Legs, 2; Feet, 2; Tail, 2.

SEAL POINT: Color, even pale fawn to cream, shading gradually into a lighter color on the stomach and chest. The coat color should not be gray. Points all the same shade of deep seal brown. Footpads and nose leather the same color as the points.

BLUE POINT: Coat color is to be a bluish white changing gradually to an oyster white on the stomach and chest. Points should be all the same shade of definite blue giving strong contrast of divided color. There must be no fawn in the coat. Foot pads and nose leather to be slate colored.

CHOCOLATE POINT: Body color ivory all over. Points milk chocolate color. Gray or dingy shading on the body is a fault. Foot pads and nose leather a cinnamon pink color.

LILAC POINT: Body color to be glacial white. Points, frosty gray with pinkish tone. Foot pads and nose leather mauve.

Colour Point Long Hairs

On the other side of the Atlantic, Mr. Brian Stirling-Webb, of England, has done much work with this same type of breeding. Himalayans are called Colour Point Long Hairs in England. There always have been crossings of Siamese and Persians, accidental and planned. Most of those planned were pursued by persons interested in obtaining a Siamese with long hair. This type of cat did not prove to be attractive to breeders of the Siamese. The long hair spoiled the effect of the sleek lines of the Siamese body, which is part of their beauty. The Persian breeders did not take to them, either, because, although the Siamese coloring was attractive, the Siamese type was so far from the Persian standard that it nullified any interest on their part.

Mr. Stirling-Webb shared these views, until he saw a female of unknown origin which quite closely resembled a Persian with Siamese coloring. He then saw possibilities of interest in the cross, if more of the Persian-like characteristics could be intensified and only the Siamese coloring retained. He then went to work in this direction, with eventual great success, as did Mrs. Goforth.

A very simplified sketch of the mechanics involved to attain this goal follows:

Both Siamese color pattern and long hair are recessive characteristics. All the kittens of the first generation of a cross between a Persian and a Siamese will be short-haired and *not* Siamese colored. If these kittens are bred together (or to others of the same type cross), the two like recessives may or may not connect with each other. When they do, a long-haired cat with Siamese coloring will result. However, these individuals may also carry the Siamese type, so the next stage of the program is to try to fix the Persian type by mating to another good-type Persian.

The results of this next mating probably will be long-haired, but not of Siamese coloring. This generation, if bred together or with others having the same type of background, will result in some kittens that have both the wanted features of the longhair and the Siamese color. Additionally, they should have an

Seal point Himalayan male kitten owned and bred by Corol MacMillan: PERSEPOLIS MOHI. Sire: Ch. Persepolis Hannabal; dam: Persepolis Minnetonka.

Blue point Himalayan female owned and bred by Mrs. J. Goforth and Mrs. Betty Meins: CH. GOFORTH'S MONA-LISA. Sire: Goforth's Sir Diamond; dam: Goforth's Mona. Photo by Gordon Laughner.

improvement toward Persian type, due to the increasing proportion of Persian in the mixture.

When making the original cross, it is well to choose a Siamese with exceptionally strong blue eye color, as the continued crosses with the Persians usually are made with the Blacks or Blues, whose copper eye color tends to dilute the desired deep blue to a pale shade.

If you can start with a Siamese that has poor Siamese type—round head, short body, short tail, etc., but good eye color, so much the better. The use of a Black Persian in the cross tends to produce good Seal Point coloring. The Blue Persian seems to give better type to the mixture. Some kittens with blue points will appear, particularly when a Blue Point Siamese is in the line of breeding. Himalayan kittens are born white and develop their color points later, as do the Siamese.

A good Himalayan or a Colour Point Long Hair, is a spectacular animal, combining as he does the particular beauty of the Persian type with the lovely contrast of the Siamese coat coloring and blue eyes. To produce such a specimen is not easy, but many enthusiastic breeders believe the result is well worth the trouble.

277

SEMI-LONGHAIRS

Maine Coon Cats

The Maine Coon Cats are haphazardly-bred longhairs. Their ancestry goes back to the 1850's, when seafaring men brought many beautiful cats to Maine from foreign ports. The Maine climate proved favorable to them, and all types of plain or fancy cats were permitted to breed at random.

The natives of Maine took great pride in their cats. They considered them bigger, better, and smarter than any other cats in the world. They soon became "natives," developing a thick coat as protection against the rugged Maine winters. They are found in all the solid colors—white, black, blue, and red (or orange)—as well as tabby. Intermingling has produced mixed coloration, often marked with white. Smokes and Silvers are rare.

After more than a century, these long-haired Coon cats continue to grace the Maine scene abundantly. The relatively recent practice of altering pet cats seems to offer the first noticeable threat to the production of surplus Coon kittens. Because they carry mixed blood strains and have no registered pedigrees, Coons are not recognized by the cat fancy, but their beauty, intelligence, and cleverness insure their popularity as pets. Since virtually all of them are born in private homes, and little can be predicted about them before they are born, locating a specific Coon kitten available for adoption depends largely on chance.

Maine Cats were the first show cats in the United States. No definite records are available, but it is known that exhibitions were held as early as the 1860's, centered principally in Maine.

The Central Maine Cat Club was organized in 1953 and now holds a show every year, in May, at Skowhegan, Maine. Usually seventy-five to one hundred cats and kittens are shown. From these (neuters included), a Maine State Champion Coon Cat is chosen for that year. The purebred cats are welcome to attend

Solid Tiger Maine Coon neuter owned and bred by Mrs. Robert Whittemore: 1958 MAINE STATE CH. TIGER BOY (NEUTER).

the show, but they cannot compete against the Coon Cats.

Mrs. Robert Whittemore, Augusta, Maine, has the only cattery that raises Coon kittens. She tells us about these unusual Maine cats:

"The Coon comes in every color, but black and white are the most common. I choose trying to specialize in solid-color Coons. My breeding stock includes: white, black, yellow (cream to red), gray (silver to blue), tiger, and calico. I cannot, however, keep supplied with all colors in either sex to meet all the specific requests received. Customers who have several color choices, and can be happy with either sex, stand a much better chance of finding a good pet promptly. Male or female kittens, I feel sure, make equally rewarding pets. At maturity, either sex may normally have gold or green eyes, and will weigh from ten to fourteen pounds.

"The Coon Cats, of course, are longhairs, but they are not as long-haired as the Persians. The fur is inclined to be thick and a little shaggy, like that of a Collie dog. Their faces are rather long and pointed, although there are some whose heads are more rounded. Their tails are long and bushy, often striped. A Coon cat stands taller than a Persian and is longer, more like the old-time Angora.

"Blu Boy 2nd, one of mine, has an interesting personality. He is very smart, loves to retrieve, rolls over, and enjoys a ride in the family car every day. He is also trained to walk with a collar and leash. He likes beef kidneys particularly well, and weighs sixteen pounds."

Long-Haired Household Pets

As previously noted in the section on shows, the household pet also has his place in the competition. Their class is divided into long-haired and short-haired varieties. They are also entered in the appropriate Speciality Show, as well as in the All Breed.

Solid Grey Maine Coon owned and bred by Mrs. Robert Whittemore: MAINE 1961 STATE CH. BLU BOY 2nd (NEUTER).

Solid White Maine Coon owned and bred by Mrs. Robert Whittemore:
1956 MAINE STATE CH. MAJOR SNO SHEEN (NEUTER).

Black and White Neuter household pet owned by June H. Bishop: JERE-MIAH JUJUBEE. Mixed Persian, ancestry unknown. Photo by Hans Bomskow.

Many persons have a special interest in seeing that these representatives of the workings of nature without human intervention get their just due. Lovely rosettes and trophies are donated for the Best Male and Best Female.

There is no standard for judging household pets. They are compared for beauty, personality, and the prime condition of their fur, which reflects their good health and their owner's devoted care. As it is unlikely that any two are exactly the same in coloring, it may be said that each cat usually is qualified to compete for a First ribbon and a Best of Color.

In some ways it is a fun class for judges, as this is the only time they can give an award to the particular cats who just plain appeal to them, regardless of their color or type. In other ways it is hard, for only one cat can be awarded the top honors, and each entrant's owner is convinced that his is *really* the nicest. However, there is surprisingly good sportsmanship shown by both the disappointed losers and the happy winners.

The judging of the Household Pets always has a large audience of spectators who root along with the exhibitors for their favorite contenders.

Our favorite contender is my sister's cat, Jeremiah Jujubee. The pride of Dearheart, his coat is rather long-haired, thick, and soft as ermine. He has been a consistent winner over his local competition for Best Household Pet.

His exhibit cage is decorated in black and white to match his black and white coloring, with a red rug on the floor to go with the red name locket which hangs from his red velvet collar. He is visited by his many fans, some of whom attend the shows especially to see him again. He is particularly interesting to the general public not only on account of his nearly perfect black and white markings but also because he looks just like the cat that they, themselves, have at home, or had at one time.

He and many other beautiful cats are the representatives of the bulk of our cat population. These "just housepets" do not have to meet any rigid standards, but they are beloved and cared for just as well as their more glamorous relatives, the pure bred longhairs and shorthairs.

This is one place where mixed ancestry is an advantage; in fact, any household pet that resembles a purebred cat too closely is not even permitted to compete in this category.

INDEX